GET THAT JOB

Joan Fletcher

Second Edition

Northcote House

First published in 1987 by Northcote House Publishers Ltd,
Plymbridge House, Estover Road, Plymouth PL6 7PZ,
United Kingdom. Tel: Plymouth (0752) 705251. Telex: 45635.
Fax: (0752) 777603.

Second edition 1991.

British Library Cataloguing in Publication Data
Fletcher, Joan *1930*
   How to get that job. — 2nd ed.
   1. Job hunting — Great Britain
   I. Title
   650.140941

   ISBN 0-7463-0617-2

Typeset by The Bemrose Press
Printed and bound in Great Britain by
Dotesios (Printers) Ltd, Trowbridge, Wiltshire.

Contents

Introduction

In today's society, there are often too many young people chasing too few jobs and the competition is fierce. Consequently, you may think "What's the point in looking for a job — whenever there *is* a vacancy it is 'snapped up' by somebody with better qualifications than I've got". Well, if you *do* sit back and wait for something to come up, you may have to wait a long time for Lady Luck to smile on you. Buying this book shows you really want to work, so why not read on and find out how to make the most of yourself and take advantage of the opportunity to improve your chances of getting that job.

This book aims at helping all school leavers, as well as young people in their late teens and early twenties to get full-time employment. It should also help those young people who have been in jobs but, for some reason or other, have suddenly found themselves unemployed.

Getting that interview

The overall objective is to help you get an interview, then the job! You should find the comments helpful and informative in an up-to-date way, so that you can quickly adopt the most appropriate approach and know what services are available to help you achieve your objective. If you take the advice and develop the described skills associated with getting a job, then your efforts are more likely to be rewarded.

The contents emphasise the importance of preparing a plan of action, getting organised and knowing your job search area — whether in this country or abroad. (If you organise yourself, you stand more chance of being successful!)

Services for job-hunters

There is reference to the numerous services provided for young people — counselling facilities and opportunities for training within different types of training schemes. (You need to know what is available so you can take advantage of the situation and make the most of it!)

Techniques

Special techniques necessary for getting an interview, then the job, are described so that you can improve your communication skills — writing letters, completing application forms, expressing yourself either by telephone or in face-to-face situations. (The extent to which you will be successful in first, getting an interview and secondly, getting a job depends on how effectively you communicate!)

The contents also reflect that an employment interview is not a 'one off' situation, particularly in a business environment with (sometimes rapidly) changing technology and subsequent redundancies. Advice is given concerning the need to follow up the employment interview in a positive way by keeping contact with employment sources and developing your own job search programme, at the same time improving your communication skills.

Checklists

You will notice that at the end of each section there is a checklist which should help you organise your efforts and make it easy for you to see where you are going and what needs doing to get the best results.

There is also a list of useful addresses, together with lists of books and leaflets which might be of help to you in your job search.

If you follow the advice given in this book and make the most of every opportunity, you should be able to present yourself in the most favourable light and stand more chance of getting that job!

1
Getting Organised

Positive approach to job hunting

Getting the right job is one of the most important things in your life —
and your parents' lives! Although luck can be an important factor, you
need to improve your chances by taking the initiative and adopting a
positive approach towards finding a job. The alternative is to wait for
the right vacancy to come along, but if you do this the chances of getting
that job are limited.

Make the most of every opportunity; take advantage of the help which
is now available to young people. Of course, there are some things you
have no control over, such as the employment situation, other applicants
and interviewers. You may have had a job and been made redundant. Even
so, the fact that there are thousands of unemployed people does not
necessarily mean that you don't stand an earthly chance of getting a job.
What it should do is emphasise the importance of organising your efforts
and working out the best and most methodical way to get that job!

Job search area: local employment situation

Where you live determines employment prospects and usually the best place
to start is home. You can do casual jobs for the family and neighbours,
a part-time Saturday job. Show you *want* to work! If you do a good job,
then it increases your pocket money, enhances your reputation in the community and enables you to acquire valuable experience — an advantage
at any employment interview. Meanwhile you can find out what full-time
employment is available by 'keeping your ears pinned back', *regularly*
reading the adverts in the local newspapers, visiting your Jobcentre, contacting your Careers Officer and even considering advertising your
'labour'. The latter method is also useful if your job search area is far
away from home and/or you have some special qualities or skills which
are likely to be wanted by an employer. An example of this would be where
you had good part-time experience in grooming and exercising horses or
working on a farm during weekends and holidays and you wanted a full-

time job doing such work. Another occasion when you might need to advertise your labour would be if you wanted a special type of practical, part-time work which would fit in with your educational studies at college or university.

Radio

Your local radio may be a useful source of information, particularly if there is a **Job Line** programme which regularly gives details of vacancies, including part-time and seasonal work in your area.

The **Help Line** is another useful feature of most local radio networks. These programmes are usually well organised/planned, so that they are presented in the best possible way and good advice is available from experienced people. Most of them are backed up by informative leaflets which you can get by writing to your local radio station.

News & Views programmes

The 'News and Views' programmes should help you get to know your area as they are related to current situations. If you listen to these regularly, you should find some of them particularly helpful and time-saving in your job search. Should you wish to widen your area and improve your knowledge of the national job situation, you can listen to national programmes which are directly about employment of young people. During the present state of high unemployment, you can expect several programmes to relate to your situation. A programme which will add to your knowledge of up-to-date national policies and practice is **File on 4** (Radio 4). As these national programmes have to be planned well in advance, you should be able to find out which are the relevant ones for you to listen to by writing to the BBC. However, if you want to plan on a weekly basis, then buy the *Radio Times* and *TV Times* for details of the following week's radio and TV programmes with additional features, letters and information about current major issues.

Using television programmes

There are some television programmes which may help you in your job search. For instance, a series called **16 UP** includes issues such as job search and interviewing. You need to find out in advance about such series and also documentaries and **Action Line** programmes which will be relevant to your job search.

You may live in an area which presents a special 'Help Line' programme such as **This is your right** (Granada), in which case you can write to your local television centre for advice and relevant leaflets. This programme is particularly helpful because it also caters for deaf people by having someone communicate in sign language. There are also educational programmes, mainly on BBC2, and although some of these are linked with the Open University, you could improve skills such as conversational French/German/Spanish just by watching and listening. Similarly, although 'Daytime on Two' (BBC2, 9.15 a.m. — 3 p.m.) is mainly for schools, occasionally there is a programme such as 'Going to Work: Life and Social Skills' which you would find helpful. Also there are some useful 'News and Views' programmes for ethnic groups, such as 'Asian Magazine' and 'Gharbar'.

Broadcasting publications

If you write to the **BBC's Education Service,** they will advise you and give details of their comprehensive range of BBC publications: leaflets, books, tapes and videotapes. The other sources of information about radio and television programmes are the *Radio Times* and *TV Times.*

Using your library

If you are unemployed and have time to spare, why not visit your local library and make use of the many facilities provided to help you in your job search? Don't be put off if your library is a modern one, using new information technology such as **computer** and **microfiche** systems. You only need to ask the librarian, who will advise you, so that part of your job search is made easier and quicker. Whatever your local library is like, there will be informative **leaflets** on display, usually presented in an eye-catching way. These are for quick reference but can also, if you choose, be taken away to read at leisure or refer to at a future date.

If you want to keep up to date with local information, there is a **noticeboard** which includes information sheets about educational, training and leisure activities. There may also be relevant forms for you to take away, complete and return to the organisation concerned.

In your job search many of the books you need to refer to, such as *Directory of Summer Jobs in Britain,* are in the Reference Section, which means you will have to use them in the library. (Don't forget to take paper and pen to note the names and addresses!), the Reference Section also

includes local and regional telephone directories as well as a selection of local and national newspapers. Main libraries usually have foreign newspapers as well as some business journals such as *The Caterer* which include job vacancies in different areas of Britain.

It may be worthwhile to consider using the library on a more long-term basis, either to improve existing skills such as letter writing or to learn about new techniques. If so, you should consult the librarian, who will help you make the best use of the library's facilities.

CHECKLIST 1: GETTING ORGANISED IN YOUR SEARCH FOR A JOB

1. **Adopt a positive approach to jobhunting:**
   organise your efforts
   try not to be disheartened if there are not many full-time jobs about

2. **Do casual work for family and friends** ⎫ Show you

3. **Get a Saturday job or part-time work** ⎬ WANT work!

4. **Regularly read advertisements in local newspapers**

5. **Visit your Jobcentre:**
   plan to be quick off the mark
   follow up vacancies

6. **Consult your Careers Officer:**
   establish contacts

7. **Consider advertising yourself (your 'labour')**

8. **Listen to selected radio programmes:**
   those which will help you in your job search

9. **Find out in advance which TV programmes will help you in your job search**

10. **Make best use of your library's facilities to help you in your job search**

2
Know Your Job Search Area

Where you live in relation to work opportunities
You need to have a clear idea of the locality and work opportunities in relation to where you live. Obviously if an employer has a choice between you and someone who lives nearer the job, he/she would probably favour that person and your application could be pushed to the bottom of the pile.

If you live in a **rural area,** the opportunities for work are likely to be restricted, e.g. seasonal farm work, depending on what kind of business organisations there are. There might be a garden centre or, even better, a large company may have taken over a country mansion as its Training Centre, but in either instance there are not likely to be many full-time jobs for local young people. Generally, if you want a skilled full-time job, you will have to get away from your village and search in town or city.

Nowadays there are signposted **industrial estates,** usually to be found on the outskirts of towns and cities. Such concentrated areas of business organisations make it easier and worthwhile for you to call at their premises. If you intend to do this, it is advisable to buy a map of your locality and find out from your Council offices, library or Jobcentre where the companies are located.

There are some types of work which are always associated with certain areas. For instance, popular **tourist areas** are good sources of employment for you if you are interested in a job in catering or hotels. You can either contact individual hotels (listed in AA and RAC handbooks and Tourist Board information) or groups of hotels such as Trust Houses Forte. Perhaps the best contact would be an agency, especially if you are over 18 years old, with experience and/or skills to offer. In particular, specialist agencies are likely to have comprehensive information about employment conditions, such as accommodation provided. Most of these types of vacancies are for a season, usually the summer.

Travelling to and from work

An employer realises that if you have to spend a lot of money in travelling to and from work, then you will tend to get disheartened and look for work nearer to home. Nowadays, as the cost of travel is of prime importance, you will have to consider several options. Would you walk, cycle, go by bus or train? Would you need to make special arrangements such as getting a lift from a friend or neighbour? Might you have to consider learning to drive; getting your own 'wheels' — scooter, motorcycle, car?

WALK for regular exercise, to keep fit or because you enjoy walking. However, remember that your shoes will wear out quickly. Repairing or replacing them could be quite costly; also you'll need waterproofs to keep out the rain and snow!

CYCLE if you want the exercise and to go places the cheap way (once you have the bike). In some areas, this is pleasant and popular transport, an enjoyable way of getting to and from work. Too bad, though, if your cycle route is part of a busy road where you can't escape exhaust fumes and where cycling may be hazardous! Consider the cost of protective outer garments for bad weather; perhaps a need to carry, in waterproof container, a change of outer clothes for use when you get to work.

Use your scooter, motorcycle, car to get to work

If you are lucky enough to have your own 'wheels', you'll surely want to use them. You'll be transported to work in a flow of pride and pleasure! The bad news: cost and time involved in learning to drive; getting your vehicle, getting it on the road, keeping it there; (for scooter and motorcycle) buying appropriate protective clothing, including essential safety helmet.

Tax, insurance and **service charges** eat up your money!

Get a regular lift from friend or neighbour

If this is necessary, you will have to sort out certain things beforehand with the person concerned. For instance, are you going to pay a fixed sum of money each week or will you share costs? How much will this be in proportion to your weekly take-home pay? How reliable will the lift be? What happens if he/she is ill, or you can't get the lift for some other reason (e.g. car breakdown)? Is there a standby or alternative — what other arrangements do you need to make? Are there likely to be any snags? What about insurance cover and liability in case of accident?

GO BY BUS if the service is regular and convenient. It might be less costly if there are any **concessions** or special schemes for which you can be considered. Remember this is a changing scene. In future, as a result of government policy, most areas will depend on privately operated buses, which could alter your transport arrangements in towns and cities. If you live in the country, hard luck! The current, usually poor services, organised for shoppers rather than workers, are unlikely to continue.

GO BY RAIL if you live in an area where there are good commuter services. In some parts of the country, travel by rail is the best way of getting to work because it is quicker, more convenient, less 'hassle' and possibly cheaper (there are special schemes, such as **season tickets**).

And finally, remember
- **Cost** — how much per day/week/month?
- **Distance** — how far there and back each day?
- **Time** — when will you have to leave home?
- **Weather conditions** — will these affect your choice?
- **Independence** — will you need help to get to work?
- **Reliability** — can you be sure of being punctual?
- **Commuting** — can you save money?
- **Workmates** — do you want to travel with workmates?
- **Convenience** — how convenient will it be?
- **Choices** — have you considered all your options?

Employers and potential employers

You need to start by finding out from your Jobcentre which organisations in your area regularly take on young people. For instance, most large international companies have a recruitment programme and on certain dates interested school leavers are invited to apply, complete selection tests and be interviewed for only a few vacancies. Such companies may not take on many young people but they regularly recruit a few at certain times of the year.

If you are interested in a trade which involves your completing an **apprenticeship,** you need to apply to the employer as early as possible because there is usually keen competition for few places. Your Careers Officer and/or Jobcentre is likely to have a list of employers who offer apprenticeships. You could also apply personally to the small businessman, such as electrical contractor, plumber, etc.

You might find there are some local employers who have a feeling of **social commitment** to the community and, even in tough economic times, they let it be known that if possible they will employ young people. In your job search area there are also bound to be some employers who take on young people because it is cheaper to do so!

Know your Local Employers

See how well you know *your* local employers:

1. Which is the biggest firm within 15 miles?
2. What kind of jobs does it offer?
3. Which are the 10 biggest office firms?
4. Which are the 10 biggest factories?
5. What local authority employers are there?
6. Which is the biggest hospital?
7. Which is the biggest hotel?
8. Which is the biggest engineering company?
9. How do you get to the nearest Jobcentre?
10. Which companies have announced expansion schemes?
11. Which have announced redundancies?
12. Which firm would you most like to work for?
13. Is there an industrial estate?
14. Is there a Chamber of Commerce? (It would probably issue a list of member firms.)

Many companies, of different sizes, are prepared to employ young people on **Youth Training Schemes.** If you are interested, it should help you to find out which of these companies tend to offer better training. It is surprising how much information you can acquire by observing, listening and asking such questions as 'Where is the training done?' 'How long does it take to become a skilled . . .?' Organised companies with proper, formal training schemes usually publicise the fact with informative leaflets which explain in detail what is involved, how long the training will take, what skills you finish up with.

If you want to know your job search area, you should try to find out as much as you can about the potential employers. If you do this and use the information to your advantage as advised in Section 12, then you are more likely to be successful in not only getting that job but getting the right job.

CHECKLIST 2: KNOW YOUR JOB SEARCH AREA

1. Decide on your job search area
   — is it far from home? ☐

2. If looking for a special type of work
   (e.g. hotel work), contact an Agency ☐

3. Find out if any employer tends regularly
   to take on young people ☐

4. If interested in apprenticeship, apply early ☐

5. Which employers have a good reputation
   for thorough training? ☐

6. Get a map and details of companies involved
   before calling at business premises ☐

7. Check travel arrangements. Any problems? ☐

8. Know travel cost so that you can
   relate it to take-home pay ☐

3
Careers Guidance and Counselling

Careers guidance at school: the Careers teacher
Careers teachers in schools organise a wide programme of activities to help students prepare for leaving school. There are **visits** to colleges of further education, factories and offices; also **representatives** from these organisations visit schools and talk about work opportunities to groups of students. The **Careers teacher** is the link with other local education careers counselling sources (Careers Officers, Careers teachers in colleges) as well as employers in the community. You should discuss your career individually with your Careers teacher at the earliest opportunity. Remember that he/she then knows you personally and information gained from the discussion should help future counselling sessions. It also enables you to make early contacts with people who can give you careers advice and gets you thinking about the issues that you will have to decide upon when leaving school.

Careers guidance at a college of further education
The Careers teacher in a college does a similar job to the one at school. However, the extent of careers guidance varies considerably throughout the different colleges. In an active college, **careers counselling** operates on a systematic basis and is closely related to educational development programmes. Therefore you need to find out what careers counselling services are actually available at your college. If there is a leaflet explaining these services, fine! If there isn't, you should contact your Careers teacher and find out the college procedure. The college library usually has relevant leaflets and is a good place to go with queries about careers information.

- How soon could you speak to your Careers teacher?
- Where can you pick up any useful leaflets?
- What careers services are available to *you*?
- Is there more than one careers staff member?
- Have you checked the library for information?

PERSONAL RECORD FOR SCHOOL LEAVER

1. School achievements
exams passed, subjects, grades
special achievements (e.g. swimming certificates)
responsibilities — prefect, Sports Captain, etc.
copy of school report (if you have a particularly good one, it is worth getting several copies, for possible employers).

2. Personal strengths
strong points, such as good attendance, reliability,
responsibilities outside school (e.g. voluntary work, shopping for old people).

3. Work experience
any part-time jobs where you have worked during holidays or weekends — paper rounds, baby-sitting, fruit/vegetable picking, community work, etc.

4. Interests
even if you think there's nothing special about your interests, it is worthwhile considering in what way they may help *you* to decide the type of job for which you may be suited and the sort of organisation you would fit into
Example: C.B. radio; help father with D.I.Y. jobs (C.B. radio reflects practical person with more than general interest, possible for apprenticeship, training in electronics)

Careers Officer

Your local Careers Officer is a most important link between education and employment. At best he will give you careers advice so that there is more chance of (a) finding a job and (b) staying in that job because you are suited to it. You might live in a place where most local employers will not interview school leavers unless arrangements have been made through the Careers Officer. When this happens, it is the Careers Officer, and possibly the Careers teacher, who does some **pre-selection.**

Whatever your situation, you need to be realistic. Try to remember that when the Careers Officer interviews you, you are one out of hundreds of young people, most competing for a few jobs or further training. Often the Careers Officer doesn't have much time to interview you and he will rely on your school report. Therefore it is essential you provide him with a copy of this, together with a prepared **C.V.** including interests and two names and addresses for **references.** You should be prepared to discuss your strong points. Make sure you don't lose your copy of the completed careers interview form, a useful document to be used for discussion with other careers counsellors. If you need further training the Careers Officer can advise and make arrangements for you to go on a Youth Training Scheme (YTS). Remember:

- Be realistic
- Organise yourself in advance
- Get a copy of your school report
- Have your C.V. ready
- Keep your own copy of the careers interview form
- Be fully prepared, and make the most of this important opportunity

Private vocational guidance agencies

Whilst discussing your career with parents and/or relatives and friends, you may consider the possibility of using a private vocational guidance agency. Some of these organisations are well established and recognised by educational authorities, others advertise nationally in papers such as

The Telegraph at appropriate times (e.g. summer holiday period). Most organisations are located in Southern England, in or near London. There are a few others in some cities but these tend to specialise in a particular aspect of careers counselling, e.g. C.V. writers. Many of the national organisations deal with students who fail their 'GCSE' or 'A' levels.

Such an organisation would give you comprehensive vocational guidance for a sometimes large fee. You would be expected to complete vocational aptitude tests and searching interviews. You need not take the advice but at least you finish up knowing more about your potential and can consider all aspects of further education and training.

Help from parents, relatives and friends

Whatever your circumstances, it is always worth considering the views of your parents, relatives and friends because usually they know you for what you are and love you for your weaknesses as well as your strengths. Although their opinions may conflict with yours, their knowledge, experience and contacts could be very helpful.

CHECKLIST 3: CAREERS GUIDANCE/COUNSELLING

1. If at school or college, see
   Careers teacher at the earliest opportunity ☐

2. If at college, find out
   Careers Counselling procedure ☐

3. Visit your library, consult librarian about
   careers information in books, etc ☐

4. See your local Careers Officer and take with
   you C.V., copy of school/college report and
   written, up-to-date personal details ☐

5. Discuss your career with your parents (and
   possibly certain relatives/friends) ☐

6. Consider getting careers counselling from a
   private vocational guidance agency
   (remember you'll have to pay for this!) ☐

4
Using Employment and Training Services

Employment and Training Services

During the last decade employment and training have been considerably influenced by changing conditions of employment and improved information technology. So much so that today, if you visit one of the new, main employment offices (e.g. Sheffield), you are bound to be impressed, possibly a bit overawed, by the 'hive' of information being processed and the 'swarms' of people communicating in different situations. You will find a wealth of **information** on display; masses of explanatory **leaflets** (some quite colourful and appealing) all about

- numerous training activities
- courses
- skills
- employment details
- vacancies
- job search advice.

However, you may not be so lucky in your part of the country. Perhaps your Jobcentre does not seem to have all these facilities, or maybe the helpful advice and support is less than you expected. If so, it is worthwhile finding out which is the main employment office in your area by looking in your local telephone directory. If you fully explore all the facilities, you will realise how important a role the Jobcentre plays in your life when you are one of several thousand unemployed young people.

Of course, if your Jobcentre *is* well organised, with easily accessible information and supportive staff who discuss and advise in a most helpful way, then it is *up to you* to make the best possible use of their services!

Jobcentres

When you visit a Jobcentre, you need to know up-to-date details of

- job vacancies
- whom to contact
- what to do so that you may be considered for the respective job.

If your Jobcentre gets news of vacancies and quickly displays them, then you can get speedily into action, there is no delay and you get a better chance of being considered for the job. After all, it may be a case of first come, first served!

So that this information can be quickly available, the staff will try to maintain fairly close contact with local employers, to whom they can offer free services such as interview facilities and advice on employment problems. From your point of view, the extent to which this contact operates successfully will depend on how helpful the services are. For instance, you will not be impressed if you visit the Jobcentre each day and see the same adverts — no change. If you receive a telephone call requesting you to attend interview, you may take a dim view of the fact that 20 other people have also been directed by the same staff to attend! What might you think if you found that particular job was filled three days ago? If you *do* have an unfortunate experience with one of the Jobcentres, don't let it put you off. Whatever the circumstances are, the facilities are there for you to make the best use you can of them. When everything and everybody works well, the whole set-up goes with a zing!! If the Jobcentre staff do their work by putting suitable people in touch with prospective employers, local companies are more likely to co-operate. The system works, there is a smooth flow of communication and everyone is happy — particularly *you* if you get the job!

Jobclubs

If you live in an area of high unemployment, you may find that there is a Jobclub. This exists to provide a place for people who have been unemployed for at least 6 months to get together to work at finding a job. The Jobcentre controls things and a member of its staff acts as leader and counsellor. There are usually about 20 members at any one time and the aim is to get each member fixed up with an appropriate job in the shortest possible time. Members stay on as long as it takes to get a job and they have to commit themselves to attending every session (at least 4 mornings each week).

Jobclubs — Do You Know . . .

- The address of the Jobclub nearest to your home?
- Its telephone number?
- The name of the organiser?
- The opening hours?
- How many members it has?
- Whether you know any members yourself?
- Whether the Jobclub produces an information leaflet you could get?
- Whether it can put you in touch with *other* Jobclubs in other localities?
- The times when it meets?
- What activities it offers?
- Whether you qualify to join?

The Jobclub leader shows members the best way to **contact employers** and make **job applications.** If you joined the Jobclub, you would be expected to carry out the advice given by using the facilities provided and contacting employers to apply for jobs. It is important to realise that all the resources, including telephone, paper, pen, envelopes, stamps and use of photocopier are FREE!

If you are interested, contact your Jobcentre who will make the necessary arrangements for you to join. However, do not be downhearted if you have to wait a while.

Training: training advisers, vocational guidance
This is the area which changes according to employment needs and current government policy about the whole aspect of people at work and the country at work. Sometimes the name of a particular course will change, even though the associated skills are the same. Sometimes the government will identify a particular national problem and inject £X million into a special project such as, recently, youth training. In that case, new type courses emerge, so it is important for you to be aware of this possibility.

When an employer says 'I'm really looking for someone with a bit more experience' it must be frustrating if you happen to have left school several months ago, applied for dozens of jobs and not been considered, even though the vacancies have been for a 16-18 year old. Well, if you can't get a job to get the experience, you can have a go at **acquiring skills** of some sort.

You may not have much idea of the kind of work for which you might be suitable, or you may fancy what appear to you to be entirely different types of jobs (outdoors or in a shop). Then again, your ideas keep changing because of what other people have said to you. You know the sort of remark 'Why don't you go in for a steady trade like a plumber — you'll always be in work'. Or someone desperate to be helpful (often one of your parents) says 'I can get you an interview at our place — it's quite good work really'. Good advice, but what really matters is that you know what you might be capable of doing and what kind of skills you can acquire in a planned way. Otherwise you could be running round in circles getting nowhere fast!

If you want to acquire new skills or improve those you have, you should see what the employment and training services can offer you. Not only can you find out about the different courses but experienced staff will give you an in-depth **interview** and advise what is most appropriate for YOU. You will be able to get free, up-to-date advice and information about any aspect of your career development and job search.

Skillcentres

Skillcentres were originally set up throughout Britain by the Government to provide intensive skills training of up to one year for people over 19 years old on a Training Opportunities Scheme (TOPS). All Skillcentres now operate as privately run establishments and local business people help to direct the training. At the same time, people receive financial help from the government in the form of training allowances, travel costs and other assistance.

Which type of course would help YOU most?

☐ Office work   ☐ Carpentry   ☐ Factory work
☐ Secretarial skills   ☐ Plumbing   ☐ Community caring
☐ Book-keeping   ☐ Electrical skills   ☐ Vehicle servicing
☐ General catering   ☐ Plastering   ☐ Electronics
☐ Bakery   ☐ Computer skills   ☐ Other
☐ Food service   ☐ Data processing
☐ General building   ☐ Business studies

● Have *you* got a leaflet from your local Skillcentre?
● What other courses are available?

The number of Skillcentres and the training skills involved differ according to the area and job opportunities. You will be able to find names and addresses in your local telephone directory but if you wish for more information it is advisable to contact your Careers Officer or Jobcentre.

When you agree to complete a specific course, your Careers Officer will make the necessary arrangements with the Skillcentre concerned. During your training, you will be responsible to a **Supervisor** in the same way you would in any formal work situation.

At the end of the course, although you won't have the depth of skills and experience that you would on a complete apprenticeship scheme, you will achieve some skills and you may pass some educational examination. You will have done something constructive and any prospective employer will be able to see evidence of your training.

What would YOU gain from a Skillcentre course?

☐ Work experience
☐ Having proper training
☐ Trying new skills
☐ Meeting new people
☐ Getting a qualification
☐ Practice in taking tests
☐ Learning to use new equipment
☐ Giving me something worthwhile to do
☐ Getting a reference for a future employer
☐ Helping me decide on a new career

Enterprise Allowance Scheme

If you are over 18 years old, unemployed (having been so for 13 weeks) and plan to set up your own business, you might wish to consider the EAS. This is a government support scheme which helps by paying you £40 per week for 52 weeks, during that difficult stage whilst you are trying to get established. Before you can apply to be considered for the EAS you must be able to show that you have available at least £1,000 which you are prepared to invest in your business over the first 12 months. Also your proposed business, which should be new, independent and small, must be approved by the Employment Service as being suitable.

Obviously, as a lot of money is involved, there are thorough procedures for getting approval. If you are interested and can fulfil the above-mentioned requirements, you should contact your local Jobcentre who will advise you and give you an **explanatory leaflet** about the scheme.

Initially you have to get information and counselling from local businessmen who have a wide experience of setting up new enterprises, and someone from the Department of Trade and Industry's **Small Firms Service** (in Wales/Scotland the Welsh/Scottish Development Agency). You then complete an application form and return it to the Jobcentre. If satisfactory, you will be interviewed by someone from the EAS teams. If your application is successful, you both sign an agreement and your weekly Enterprise Allowance starts. Afterwards there are periodic checks by the EAS team.

CHECKLIST 4: MAKING FULL USE OF THE FACILITIES PROVIDED BY THE THE EMPLOYMENT TRAINING SERVICE

1. Get to know what facilities are available ☐

2. Ask for relevant written information, including leaflets, to take away and consider at your leisure ☐

3. Ask for an in-depth interview and vocational guidance ☐

4. Act quickly on any information given to you by the Employment Training staff ☐

5
Getting Onto Training Schemes

You can formally acquire skills and get work experience by completing one of the several government-funded training schemes. As these are modified from time to time, you will need to keep your information up-to-date.

Youth Training
During the past few years, Youth Training schemes have been available for a period of up to 1 year but from now on, as a school leaver, you will be eligible for up to 2 years training. If you are **disabled,** you can join the scheme up till you are 21 years old. Otherwise, if you are over 18 years old, you qualify for employment training. If employed, it is possible to do a youth programme as part of your training plan but you are more likely to be interested if you haven't got a job. This is because if you are accepted for it, you will have a programme of **planned work experience,** further education and off-the-job training, all specially designed to help you prepare for work in an area that you are interested in.

On Youth Training, you would gain

- **work experience** from more than one employer or in more than one department of a large firm.

- **off-the-job training** and continued education at either a local college or private training centre.

Thus you would learn skills relating to your work experience and prospective area of employment. During that time you would be able to get careers advice to help you make the best use of the scheme and find an opening afterwards. However, it is important for you to realise that there is no definite promise of permanent employment at the end of the scheme.

1st year training is organised with a group of similar jobs in mind, for example, several jobs that occur in an office. Additionally, you will be able to acquire skills that will be useful in most jobs as well as life outside work. Such skills would involve using computers, solving problems and communicating clearly with other people.

If you are eligible for further training — up to 2 years — the 2nd year will involve training in specific skills. For instance, if you did general training in office work in the 1st year, you would train specifically as, say, an Accounts clerk during the 2nd year.

- If you join the Youth Training at 17 years old and have completed one year at school or college on a full-time training course related to the area of work which interests you, you may be able to go straight into the 2nd year of the scheme.

Although many different organisations, such as local training agencies and local employers, arrange Youth Training Schemes, it is usually the Careers Officer who plays an important role in co-ordinating such schemes. He/she will advise you and make the necessary arrangements in a formal way so that if you decide to complete a scheme, your local training programme will be agreed at the beginning. You will receive an explanatory letter **(Training Agreement)** which includes details of your obligations and what you can expect in terms of holiday arrangements, hours of work, etc. At the end of the Scheme you will receive a **certificate** showing your achievements, experience and training, as well as 'off-the-job' training and any examinations passed (e.g. RSA Typing Stage II, C & G Design). This certificate could

- provide useful information to a prospective employer who will tend to use it as a basis for discussion of your experience and achievements

- give you the opportunity to acquire skills and experience in preparation for work whilst you are searching

- prove your worth to an employer so that, although he is not able to offer you permanent employment, he can recommend you and give you a good reference.

Certificate of Pre-Vocational Education (CPVE)
If you are a school leaver with poor to modest examination results, your main aim is to get a job! Unfortunately, you are likely to be in competition with hundreds of other young people who have good examination results. Your problem may be made worse by the fact that you have not

yet formed a clear idea of the kind of job you could tackle successfully. Or you may not be ready to start a specific course or training scheme such as BTEC or Youth Training. If you fit into one or more of these categories, you should consider a CPVE course.

What is involved in a CPVE course?

You would attend a one-year course at either school or college. The school/college designs its own particular course, based within a nationally-agreed framework of CORE LEARNING AREAS and VOCATIONAL SKILLS covering such things as: communication skills; numeracy; practical skills; creative development; social skills; personal and career development.

Should you decide to do this CPVE course, your learning situation and programme will be negotiated by you and the Course Organiser; consequently you should benefit by having a personalised programme. There is the added advantage that when you complete the year's course, you gain a nationally-recognised certificate which should enable you to further your education and training. As this is a new type of course, you may be lucky or unlucky, depending on what is available in the particular area where you live. If you are interested in CPVE you should contact your Careers teacher or Careers Officer who will advise you.

Employment Training

There is so much redundancy these days and an increasing number of firms going 'bust' that it is quite common for people over 18 years old suddenly to find themselves unemployed. If you have to face this situation you are likely to ask yourself whether you should **update the skills** you already have or get training in new skills. Whatever you decide, you will need to know how you would benefit from going on an Employment Training Scheme. If accepted on this scheme, you would be able to get basic training or up-dating in a wide variety of skills covering craftwork, office work, computing, technician and management work. It would open up job opportunities in many industries.

Most of these courses last 3 — 6 months full-time, although a few involve one year's training. Unless you are disabled, the maximum duration of Employment Training is one year in any three-year period. Your course is most likely to be held locally, at a college or employer's premises or a Skillcentre. However, it could be held at one of the few regional centres, in which case you would be involved in considerable travelling or have to live away from home. In either instance, the **costs** would be paid by the Employment/Training Service.

These courses are often advertised in national newspapers and journals.

TAPS (Training Access Points)

You will be able to take advantage of recent developments in computer technology and get quick access to wide-ranging information about education and training for all kinds of skills at every level. This TAPS service is available at your Jobcentre, Careers Office, library and possibly at other locations such as the Training Commission Area Office or Inner City Employment Office.

Community Projects

If you are

- aged 18-24,
- unemployed and have been so for the last 2 months
- out of work for at least 6 of the last 9 months
- read on!

You may not have won a prize but you *have* become eligible to join a Community Project which gives you a chance to work either full or part-time for up to one year on a project which is helping the local community. You would be paid whatever the local hourly rate for the job is, for the number of hours you worked.

The duration of the project and type of work you would do would depend on what the purpose was. If you live in an area where the authorities have decided to fund a scheme involving clearing canals then that task would take a long time even if a large group of people were taking part. On the other hand, the project may be an ongoing community scheme such as running city farms or gardening and decorating for elderly and disabled people, in which case you might be accepted for short periods of employment.

Despite occasional adverse comments about this type of work (cheap labour, etc.) if you get involved you will benefit in several ways. For instance, it could be something that you have wanted to do, perhaps, for the good of the community (e.g. helping the elderly and disabled). It would keep you in the **habit of work** and you would make new friends and contacts. Your particular Community Project may also enable you to get some useful formal training, including 'off-the-job' training at your local college.

Do YOU want . . .

☐ Something worth doing?	☐ To get a reference?
☐ To keep the work habit?	☐ To get experience?
☐ To make new friends?	☐ To keep fit and active?
☐ To see new places?	☐ To hear about new jobs?
☐ To try something new?	☐ To keep earning?

Then a Community Project could be for you.

Usually you would be allowed to attend job interviews and, if offered a permanent job, you would be able to finish immediately. Whatever else, you would be paid for your work and surely that would be better than being unemployed?

Training courses for those with special needs
If you are a **young disabled person,** training can be arranged at any time after leaving school. This could include the usual Youth Training where there is a certain flexibility concerning the time factor of when you have to do the training (e.g. you may be accepted for Youth Training up to the age of 21).

In addition, there are special training opportunities:

- with an employer who is prepared to train you and employ you for at least 6 months after the training has finished
- at a residential centre which is staffed and equipped to cater for people with special needs. Consequently, a wide range of training such as computer programming is offered, depending upon the area of your interest.

The centre may be a small set-up with hostel accommodation provided, or you could attend one of the big residential centres such as St. Loyes College for Training the Disabled for Commerce and Industry, Exeter, Devon, or the Royal Blind School, Edinburgh, where courses include shorthand-typing, audio-typing and switchboard operating.

Additionally, your Local Authority may be one of those which provide **educational grants** especially for disabled people to study for the professions. If you require information and advice, contact your Disablement Resettlement Officer or, if you are under 19 years of age, your local Careers Officer.

Private Training
You, or you and your parents, may decide it will be best to acquire certain skills at a privately-run training centre. You could be the type of person who is more likely to benefit from personal, private tuition rather than by joining a group on a government training scheme. Whatever the reason, if you opt for private training, you must be prepared to pay for it.

In fact, when there is high unemployment, it may be well worth thinking about whether to spend money on intensive training in order to improve your chances of getting a job. After all, you should be successful if your private organisation has good contact with employers. Also, if your chosen private training company is well-known, then employers will be impressed by its reputation and consequently be more interested in your application.

CHECKLIST 5: TRAINING SCHEMES

1. Get to know what training schemes are
available before making your final choice ☐

2. Train to keep up with changing technology ☐

3. Make sure you know what is involved before
you commit yourself to any training ☐

4. Whilst training, work hard to obtain future
good reference and useful job contacts ☐

5. Consider paying for private, intensive training
to improve your chances of getting that job ☐

Remember that doing something constructive is better than 'hanging around' with time on your hands!

6
Advertised Vacancies

Jobcentres

Government policy determines where Jobcentres are located and the way in which they are operated. However, there is a network of local (Employment Service) offices throughout Great Britain. It is important to visit your Jobcentre regularly — not just when you happen to be near. You need to be aware of what jobs are available, not only for the moment but for future plans. For instance, you may be interested in a particular job but know that you need more qualifications and that makes you decide on a college course. If you have a query, ask the Jobcentre staff, and ensure they know you are keen to get a job as quickly as possible. Don't worry that they may think you are 'a pain'. They are more likely to put you in touch with a job just to get rid of you! The important thing is to know about *all* the vacancies, bearing in mind that it may be necessary to acquire further education or training before you can be considered for the kind of job you would like to do.

Television and local radio

Some television companies and local radio stations have regular (Jobwatch/Jobfinder) programmes which feature a selection of vacancies — most of the information being provided by the local Jobcentre. It would be worthwhile finding out about such programmes.

Advertisements

Most employers like to be selective and advertise a vacancy so that they have as wide a choice as possible (it is quite common to have two or three hundred replies to a block advert). Adverts for young people vary in size and content. Generally, block adverts are informative, reflecting what the job involves, qualifications and skills required, training, etc. Other personal requirements may be stated: 'must be smart in appearance' . . . 'have a good personality'. You should also look for the small advert which gives only brief details. It is worthwhile following this up because there may well be a super job in it for you!

CLERICAL

YOUNG PERSON
16-17 required to train as
RECEPTIONIST/CLERK
Male-Female
on YTS scheme. Must be very
keen and willing to learn.

TELEPHONE 12345

YOUNG PERSON required to operate new work control system in busy photocopying servicing department in Blankly. Must have good telephone manner and be able to record messages accurately, to receive incoming service calls and allocate calls to engineers as well as general office duties. A knowledge of the surrounding area would be an advantage. — Please telephone 12345 for an application form.

16-17 YEAR OLD. Well spoken and with minimum of 4 'O' Levels, including Maths and English is required for reception and general office duties — Written applications including CV's to Jones & Jones, Chartered Accountants, 116 Smithville Road, Smithtown. SM12 3XX (No agencies).

SECRETARIAL

ADMINISTRATOR required for company close to city centre. Position demands a confident outgoing person (male-female) with an excellent telephone manner and organisational skills. Salary negotiable. For further details contact — Janice Jones, Simon Smith Recruitment Consultants on 12345.
AN ADVANTAGE to be trained at Smithville Business College! Contact our qualified tutors and then decide. RSA-Pitman Centre. Secretarial-Computer courses Basic-Advanced. Flexi hours. 12345.
BLANKLEY TRAINING CENTRE Blankly House, 18 High Road. An RSA, Pitman, EMFEC Examination Centre. For professional courses in Teeline, Pitman 2000 and New Era Shorthand, Typewriting, Word Processing and Book Keeping (Manual & Computerised Systems) — Tel: 12345
A1 SHT AND AUDIO SECS urgently req. (male-female) for immd bookings. Top rates — Contact Smithline Agy, St. Peter's St., Smithtown. Tel 12345.
A1 TEL-REC'S req for immd assignments both in the centre and surrounding areas. Exp of Monarch, Kinsman and 4x18 flick adv. Top rates — Contact Smithline Agy, St Peter's St, Smithtown. Tel 12345.

SCHOOL LEAVER 16-17 yrs old required to train as Office Junior in a small office environment. Must be of pleasant disposition. Typing experience advantageous. — Written application only including full c.v. to Jones Limited, Midtown Offset House, Victoria Avenue, Upper Smith Street, Blankly, Smithville XX1 1XX.

SECRETARIAL

SHORTHAND TYPIST
required by Jones Ltd for their head office situated on Smithville Road, Blankly.

Applications (male-female) aged 18 plus will have obtained speeds of 80 wpm shorthand and 40 wpm typing. Experience of word processing would be advantageous. Salary £4,680 rising to £4,968 after 6 months.

Please apply in writing to the
PERSONNEL MANAGER
JONES LIMITED
243 SMITHVILLE ROAD
BLANKLEY
SMITHTOWN
XX1 1XX
Giving full details of age, qualifications and experience

JOIN A WINNING TEAM
SALES OFFICE ASSISTANT
Male-Female

Required to provide back up services to our Sales Liaison and Marketing Services division. Typing/filing/sales statistics. Scope to work on own initiative. Word processing skills advantageous but not essential as training will be given. Previous office experience essential. Ideally aged 18-25 years.

Telephone Tony Smithson
SMITHTOWN 12345

THE SMITHTOWN CLUB
Exclusive City Centre Club

requires full time day
RECEPTIONIST

He-she will be aged 21 years plus, with approximately 2-3 years experience in typing, switchboard work an advantage.

A pleasant personality and ability to deal with people essential. This is a demanding job which requires tact, efficiency and an ability to cope under pressure as well as a sense of humour.

Excellent references essential, good salary, 4 weeks holiday per annum, lunches provided.

Please apply in own handwriting giving full details of career to date enclosing a photograph.

Miss M. Jones, The Smithtown Club, 16-20 Smithville Road, Smithtown.

Typical advertisements . . .

NANNY
REQUIRED

Preferably to live in, Blankly area. To care for two children, aged 2 and 1 year. Experience preferred. With references.

Telephone BLANKLY 12345

BLANKLY TRAINING GROUP

Are looking for 16 to 17 year olds, who are interested in an agricultural career. Excellent prospects, guarantee of full time position or full time Agricultural College for the successful applicant at the end of 2 years training on YTS.

Tel, Mrs Jones, Blankley 1234

YOUNG STRONG LAD required for potato harvesting — Tel. Lower Blankley 1234.

HAIR-LINES OF BLANKLY
require a
QUALIFIED HAIRSTYLIST
or
SECOND YEAR
IMPROVER
Telephone
Blankly 12345 daytime
or Smithtown 1234
evening

LIFT ENGINEERS ASSISTANT
required

Aged 18/19 (male/female) with at least two years Engineering experience. Ex YTS acceptable. Preference given to those who have already achieved first year College Certificate.

Successful applicant would assist Senior Engineers with Lift Installations throughout the Midlands area.

Please ring:
SMITH & JONES LIMITED
Smithtown 12345
for application form.

TRAINEE EXAMINER

Position would suit school leaver. Required for work on High Fashion Hosiery. If you feel that this is the job for you **Phone Blankly 12345** to arrange an interview.

EUROPEAN-AMERICAN HOSIERY LIMITED
2 Smith Road, Blankly,
Smithtown XX1 1XX.

AB LIMITED JEWELLERS offer YTS/ECTT trainee position for 16 year old school leaver. Applicants should have good level of Maths and English education and will be given full basic training into retail jewellery. Apply in writing only, AB Limited, 12-14 Smith Street, Blankley.

SHOP ASSISTANT Required (full time) for fruit and veg. Must be of smart appearance. Wages and hours details upon application. — Telephone 12345 between 9am and 5.30pm.

16-17 YEAR OLD PERSON Required to train in all aspects of ladies and gentlemans hairdressing. Career minded applicants only please. — Apply in writing to Mrs I. Jones, The Hairdressers, 2, Blankley Street, Smithtown.

MOTHERS HELP/Au Pair, central Blankely. Live in 5 days minimum. Non-smoker. Children 5 and 6 years. Normal household duties — Tel 1234. References essential.
WANTED DOMESTIC HELP, Blankely, 6 hours per week, hours by arrangement. Tel — Blankely 12345.

NNEB NANNY REQUIRED
BLANKLY EDGE AREA
Live-out

For baby expected in November.
and for Thomas, aged 5
Car driver
Good references
essential

Tel. Blankely 12345

TRAINEE Fabric examiner 16 to 17 years old. Some heavy work involved. Contact — Mr B Smith on 12345 Smith' Knitting Company.

PRINTING TRAINEE We have a vacancy for a Printing Trainee on a YTS Scheme. Applicants should be 16/17 years old and adaptable. Small family firm in Blankely. — Tel. 12345

BUTCHERY TRAINEES required. Full training given but some experience preferred. Tel 12345
CARE/DOMESTIC ASSISTANT required for small residential home. YTS appointment leading to full time position. Tel. 12345

TWO 16 to 17 YR OLDS Required, one as trainee butcher, one as general grocery assistant. YTS — Tel 12345 Mrs Smith AM only.
WANTED Experienced senior sales assistant, YTS position available. — Apply Smithfayre, 35, Blankely Street, Smithtown.

...think how you would apply for one of these jobs.

Hearsay — friends, relatives

In many places, usually small communities, informal communication has considerable influence regarding job prospects. Word gets passed around that there may be a job going at . . . Frequently, jobs are 'found' as a result of chat over a glass of beer or a cup of coffee, although perhaps it isn't as easy for that to happen these days because of the tough economic situation. Also, there are still some organisations which, as a matter of company policy, advertise within the company first, in order to encourage friends and relatives to apply. You should quickly follow up any hearsay, but remember that there may *not* be a job or possibly there *is* a job but you are not suitable. The main thing is to keep trying and one day you may be lucky!

Which of these have *you* tried?

- ☐ Asking all your family and relatives?
- ☐ Asking your neighbours?
- ☐ Asking your own friends and acquaintances?
- ☐ Asking school or college friends?
- ☐ Asking teachers and lecturers you know?
- ☐ Asking any business people you know?
- ☐ Asking at any clubs you belong to?
- ☐ Writing to anyone?
- ☐ Asking any other friends in work?

Educational sources — school, college, local Careers Officer

If you live in an area where the careers guidance services are most active, there will be strong **links with local employers.** At school, employers or their representatives will talk to groups of students about opportunities in their organisations and interviews will be arranged. At your college of further education, there is likely to be much closer liaison with employers.

When Careers teachers are informed of vacancies, they will pass the information on to the students, then arrange interviews and supply college references. Your local Careers Officer provides the most important source of known vacancies for young people, particularly since the advent of Youth Training Schemes.

Who is my local Careers Officer?

NAME _____

ADDRESS _____

_____

_____

PHONE _____

If all these educational services work smoothly and efficiently, you could be one of many young people who get jobs for which they are likely to be most suited.

Private Employment Agencies

Most of these, particularly the national bureaux, are located in cities and large towns. Generally speaking, private agencies do not cater for young people, unless they have some special skill or experience to offer. Exceptions to this would be those agencies which deal with residential domestic work, including assistant nursery nursing, either in this country or abroad (if abroad, applicants must be over 18 years old). If you *do* have some skill or experience, it is always advisable to contact these private employment agencies in order to keep up-to-date with the employment situation. They may also put you in touch with part-time employment.

Some agencies located in Port areas deal with applications for those wishing to **work at sea.** If you are interested in such a career, there are opportunities to become a trainee with a private shipping company or join the Merchant Navy. You don't need formal academic qualifications to be a Deck rating, although 'O' levels would be useful. However, if you wish to become an Officer, you will need at least five 'O' levels. When accepted, you will be able to progress through the Officer grades by experience and successfully taking exams for higher grades. Needless to say, if you wish to work at sea, good health and fitness are essential requirements. Also, if you intend working in the general manning of a ship, you must have perfect colour vision without glasses or contact lens.

Work in H.M. Services

If you like the idea of travel, training and good pay — all within a disciplined life, then you should consider joining one of Her Majesty's Services — the Navy, Army or Air Force.

All three Services have Careers Information Offices located throughout the country and if you are considering such a career, you should write to the nearest one (address in local telephone directory). You should bear in mind that there are not as many openings in the Navy and Air Force. Also, you need some 'O' levels and/or CSEs Grade 1 to support your application. In both these Services, there are different schemes of entry depending on your academic qualifications.

Generally, there are more opportunities in joining the Army and the different schemes of entry depend on your aptitude as well as age and qualifications (you don't need academic qualifications for some schemes of entry and will be accepted providing you pass certain aptitude tests, a thorough medical examination and interviews).

Young men 16-17½ yrs old

If you have a flair for music, you can apply to be a Junior Bandsman. As well as being taught to play an instrument, if you have exceptional musical talent, you could get a year's course at the Royal Military School of Music. On the other hand, you might think you have leadership qualities and want the opportunity to develop those at an early age. If so, you should apply to be considered as a Junior Leader. Perhaps you fancy being trained as a technician or craftsman? If so, you can apply for Junior entry as an Apprentice technician or craftsman and be trained in 2 years at the Apprentice College. If you are over 17 yrs old, with at least five 'O' levels, you could be considered for the School entry for Regular Commissions.

Young women over 17 yrs old

You can join either the (a) WRAC and be trained for one of a variety of jobs such as driving, clerical, technical, etc *or* (b) QARANC and be trained for one of a few non-nursing jobs, including clerical and laboratory technician work.

If you are interested in any Branch of the Services, you should write to the nearest Service Careers Information Office. You will be invited to attend interview, complete several selection tests and undergo a thorough medical examination. If successful and depending on your entry scheme, you will be required to sign on for a specified number of years, with an option to leave the Service after a certain time.

Professional & Executive Recruitment (PER)

This national organisation, now the biggest of Britain's recruitment consultants, assists anyone who enrols to find a suitable job. You can **enrol** for a fee and benefit from a wide range of advice, including up-to-date information about vacancies, the job market, job search techniques, support services, details of available courses and self-help groups; also skills in presenting yourself in the best way. You would be sent a free weekly **jobs newspaper** and informed of any aspect concerning local employment which would affect your job search plan.

PER tends to be used by qualified and/or experienced people. For instance, if you are a newly qualified graduate, you would be sent the weekly

Graduate Post. If you are an experienced person over 20 years old, you would be sent the *Executive Post.* Each newspaper usually gives details of several hundred vacancies across the entire range of professional occupations, so you can imagine just how useful this information would be to you when developing your personal job search programme.

You would also be kept up-to-date with national employment news and special features, as well as information about **training courses** and advice about **self-employment.**

CHECKLIST 6: KNOWN VACANCIES

1. Visit Jobcentre frequently ☐

2. Read local newspaper advertisements regularly ☐

3. Don't overlook the small adverts ☐

4. Study the adverts carefully. See what is needed: do you match up to job requirements? ☐

5. Decide how to reply — letter, phone or call at business premises ☐

6. If you hear of a (possible) vacancy, follow up without delay ☐

7. When educational sources (school, college, Careers Officer) publicise vacancies, follow up immediately ☐

8. If appropriate, consider using the services of private employment agencies ☐

9. Keep up-to-date with the employment situation; get to know the job market ☐

7
Writing Application Letters

Making an impact on paper

An employer will be influenced by what he/she *sees*:

- the general appearance of your letter of application
- type of paper used
- layout and presentation
- legible writing
- balanced paragraphs.

Then he/she will be further impressed upon reading the contents: is the meaning clear, with good sentence construction, correct spelling and appropriate punctuation? Is the information organised? Are the comments relevant? (Do not expect an employer to have either time or inclination to read irrelevant comments, however interesting they may be!) Avoid being too lengthy, at the same time ensuring that your comments reflect a clear overall impression of you in relation to the job. Aim to write a letter of application which has the qualities of a good business letter, yet is individualistic, revealing your strengths.

Paper, pen and writing

Most employers ask you to apply in writing. Avoid using lined paper, however tempting it may be to do so, especially if your handwriting is big and sprawly, or if you tend to write sloping instead of straight across the page of unlined paper. An employer will favour good quality, unlined paper and often not bother to read lined paper. If you decide to use good quality coloured paper, please consider the reaction of the reader (perfumed, lilac-coloured paper from a young man may well be misinterpreted!)

It is also important to consider the type of pen you use as this will influence your writing. Obviously you will know which type of pen will produce your best, most legible writing.

6 Pear Tree Drive
Balmuir
BK9 2AO

Dear Mr Johnson,   8th April 86

Will you please consider me for a suitable vacancy within your organisation.

I am 18 yrs old and will be finishing a 2 yr Business Studies (BTEC) National Diploma Course this June. During the course, I have been able to do part-time work, weekends and holidays, working for an Estate Agent — However, I do not wish to pursue that type of work for my career.

Working for your company appeals to me because you have a good reputation for giving young people the chance to prove themselves. Also, I know several of your employees.

I enclose my C.V. and meanwhile should be grateful if you would grant me an interview.

Yours sincerely,

James Pontin.

Mr C. Johnson
General Manager
National Insurance
The Square
Balmuir   BK1

Exploratory letter — when sent with a typed C.V., this would have good impact. Comments are positive and brief. The writer knows about business format and the handwriting is legible.

Presentation: organisation of contents

The reader will be influenced by the layout of your letter. Practise writing two or three examples, and check each one:

- Is it recognised business format?
- Is the message presented so that the reader will be interested in your application?
- Are the essential facts clearly and briefly presented so that the employer does not have to search for them.

Consider how much more can be communicated by implication and, if possible, include useful information which is relevant to job requirements and will add to the 'depth' of your profile. Your comments should clearly show that you have thought about and/or found out about what the job involves and that you possess certain qualities worthy of consideration.

Exploratory letter of application

If you live in an area where there are many developing firms or large organisations, this approach can be most successful. You write this type of letter when there isn't a known vacancy but you would like to work for that particular company and believe you have something to offer. When there isn't a job, it is most important to make some impact relating to your strengths. Unless you prepare your letter carefully, you are likely to get the reply 'Thank you but . . . no vacancies'.

BURNSWELL Mary Joanne

27 Elmsworth Road

NEVERTON

Date of birth: 21 Apr 67

Nr Derby

Marital status: Single

DE90 1LN

Provisional driving licence

Telephone: Neverton 93784

EDUCATION & QUALIFICATIONS

School	From	To	Exam	Subject/Grade	
Neverton Comprehensive	80	84	'O'	English Language	C
				French	C
			+ 6 CSEs incl Maths(1); Chemistry(2)		
			RSA	Typewriting Stage I	

Further Education

Lumley College of F.E.	84 -	1yr F/T Business Studies course (BTEC)*
		incl.Data Process; People & Communication

WORK EXPERIENCE

From	To	Employer	Job responsibilities
Sep 84 Hols & Sats	- *	J Durmond & Co Engineering Derby	Typist/General Clerical Assistant Invoicing - customer queries; Relief Switchboard Operator
83 & 84 Summer Hols		Post Office/Store Neverton	Sales Assistant - helped with ordering and checking stock

INTERESTS

Home: cooking; helping mother; decorating; painting

Social: dancing; Pop concerts; belong to local Youth Club

Sports: particularly tennis; enjoy cycling; support Neverton United

REFERENCES

Mr L Smithson, General Manager
J Durmond & Co
Alton Road
DERBY DE41 8VB

TEL: Derby 61034

Ms V Hobson, Postmistress
Neverton Post Office
NEVERTON
Nr Derby DE99 1LN

TEL: Derby 410965

To get good impact, you need to present an organised, typed C.V. (**Curriculum Vitae**) together with a handwritten letter, both preferably on one side of the paper only. The handwritten letter should have correct business letter layout with three or four paragraphs. It should be legible, brief and clear, with meaningful comments reflecting your strong points. Aim to tell a prospective employer about yourself at that time and imply possible development of your strong points so that you will be regarded as worthy of consideration for employment.

If you have been made redundant, do not be afraid to give details. Redundancy should never be concealed because this would only come out at an interview and the interviewer would suspect you of hiding something. The important thing is that you have acquired work experience and, possibly, skills.

Curriculum Vitae (C.V.)

Your C.V. should be typed in order to achieve the best possible impact. Unless you are a trained typist, it is advisable to get some help with this.

Also, if it is well typed, you can get several copies of it — most useful if you have to write many letters of application.

You need to organise the details to make easy reading and presentation is vitally important so that the reader can, at a glance, see essential 'blocks' of facts. These will cover personal details, education and qualifications, experience, interests and the names and addresses of two people who would give you references. If your C.V. is well designed, it can also be a useful document for the employer to use during your interview.

Remember:

- The **typed** CV makes the best impression
- Use the CV to **say as much as you can** about yourself
- Use plenty of clear **headings**
- Make plenty of good clear **copies** for future use
- Always make sure it is **up-to-date**

CHECKLIST 7: LETTER OF APPLICATION

1. This should be as brief as possible, yet contain the information the employer requires (personal details related to the job) ☐

2. It should be clearly written on good quality, unlined paper with correct business letter layout and presentation ☐

3. The letter may have an attached C.V. stating relevant details: name, date of birth, marital status, address, telephone number, driving licence, education and qualifications, work experience, interests, references ☐

4. The 'tone' of your letter should reflect your personal profile, emphasising your strengths related to the job. When there is no vacancy, it is particularly important to make some impact relating to your strengths ☐

5. Always read through what you have written to ensure it makes sense and is accurate, brief and clear! ☐

8
Filling Up Application Forms

Use of these for selection and employment purposes
Many firms use some kind of application form to help them shortlist applicants for interview. The form can also be used as a source document (personal record) of the employee. A contract of employment is based upon the completed application form, so you can appreciate how important it is to both employer and employee.

Some large organisations have special forms for different groups of workers but generally an application form is designed for people of all ages with varying experience and qualifications. Bear this in mind when completing an application form and don't be 'put off' by questions which seem inappropriate for you.

Completion of application forms: understanding the questions
It is always necessary to read an application form carefully before you put pen to paper, so that you fully understand the questions. The company is not trying to catch you out by asking tricky questions, but sometimes there are words that you don't understand, so you may need a dictionary to find out what the question is all about.

If there is a difficult question, it is advisable to have some paper and jot down points *before* you actually write on the form. In this way it will be possible to see how the information will look. Will it be clear and in logical order? It also gives you the opportunity to check that the information is accurate *before* you commit yourself to paper.

Presentation: impact, legible writing, clear facts, logical order
Use the application form to help you present your best, true profile, with an accurate record of personal details, qualifications, skills and experience. Include redundancy details if applicable.

Make sure you include part-time work and write meaningful comments about interests (not what you think the reader will want to see on the form).

APPLICATION FORM QUESTIONS

Questions which need to be considered carefully and written down on separate paper before you complete the application form. Organise your answer — make sure comments are accurate, brief and clear!

QUESTION: State interests and hobbies including positions
or   of responsibility held.
QUESTION: Give brief details of the hobbies, sports and societies which are most important to you. Mention any offices held and any awards or distinctions you have obtained.
EXAMPLE Stamp collecting 6 yrs (most valuable stamp worth £35)
ANSWER: Football — play Sunday League; support 'X' United
Just started to learn to drive.
EXAMPLE Reading — mostly historical novels; belong to local library
ANSWER: Home — cook for family at weekends
Outdoor — walking, cycling, some birdwatching (belong RSPB)

QUESTION: Write briefly about your career to date. Refer to your achievements and ambitions. Mention any aspect which you think is important in relation to this job.
ANSWER: Your comments need to be accurate, brief and clear; in logical order so there is a good 'flow' and the reader gets a better 'picture' of you and how you see yourself in this job. Relate your strong points, experience, etc. to the job requirements.

QUESTION: State any additional information you consider relevant to your application.
ANSWER: Consider all questions (and information on C.V) — do your answers reflect a complete profile, emphasising your strengths in relation to the job? If NO, then write down missing information. Make sure your comments are relevant — do not waffle!!

Could you answer the following questions about your health?

What is your weight? _____ height? _____
Is your eyesight good/normal? _____
When did you last have a medical? _____
If you are a registered disabled person (RDP), do you know your registra-
tion number? _____ When does this need renewing? _____

Do you suffer or have you suffered from:

Diabetes   YES/NO
Heart Trouble   YES/NO
Stomach Trouble   YES/NO
Skin Trouble   YES/NO
Any Accident   YES/NO
Any Rupture   YES/NO
Any Muscle Trouble   YES/NO
Any Nerve Trouble   YES/NO

Would you know if you had suffered from such things as:
severe abdominal pains — hernia — dyspepsia — tuberculosis — rheumatic
pains — epilepsy — fibrositis — sinusitis — dermatitis — congenital defor-
mity — psychiatric problems ???

(Did you get through this without the help of a dictionary? If so, well
done!)

The usual question to check that your health is good is:
Give details of any serious illness or time spent in hospital.

Be accurate, brief and clear !!!

Consider carefully who the **referees** will be. If you can get someone
known to the company to give you a reference, it should be to your
advantage.

Try to give a full picture when you state skills and qualifications. For
instance, if you only put down 'O level Maths passed' when you have four
other 'O' levels at D grade, you must not expect the employer to be a
mindreader!

If there is not enough space on the form, you will need to write on an
extra sheet of paper. Most forms ask you to do this so that nothing
important is missed out.

**CHECKLIST 8: COMPLETING AN EMPLOYMENT
APPLICATION FORM**

1. Read all the questions carefully before
   picking up your pen ☐

2. Don't write anything on the form until you fully
   understand the question and know exactly
   what you want to say ☐

3. Use black ink (suitable for copying) ☐

4. If you are doubtful about any spelling, check
   beforehand (use a dictionary) ☐

5. Ensure that your writing is legible
   and the facts accurate ☐

6. Don't forget to sign and date the form ☐

7. Read what you have written to ensure it is accurate,
   brief and clear. If possible, get someone
   to check the completed form as well ☐

Overheard in the Personnel Department . . .

"I just couldn't read his *writing*!"

"I know what you mean. He should have used block capitals."

"One girl put her age down as 6702."

"It must have been her phone number?"

"Could be, but I think there are five digit numbers in that
town. Also, she gave her address as the YWCA. I wonder if she's
really got a permanent address?"

"That chap didn't put down a single thing under other interests
and hobbies. I thought when reading his letter he sounded a
pretty dull individual — hardly the sort of person we need
in sales."

"There was another one which was all filled in with a pale blue
felt tip pen. Unfortunately, it wouldn't photocopy for our
records department. Pity, really."

"Still, there were some good ones . . ."

"Will you let me look through them, please?"

9
Using the Telephone

Good telephone technique

The quickest way to get rejected is to telephone without thinking about what you are going to say and what you intend asking. You may enjoy telephoning and even think you are good at it, but there are so many things that can go wrong if you are unprepared. It may be that an employer wants someone with a good telephone manner, in which case the person at the other end of the line will soon 'pick up' whether or not you have really thought about the phone call beforehand. .

When using the telephone in applying for a job you should have a good technique so that time isn't wasted. Good telephone technique depends on whether you listen carefully, give essential information clearly and in logical order and the extent to which you are able to express yourself and develop a discussion about your strong points in relation to the work situation. You will be able to discuss more naturally if you find out a few details about the company *before* making the telephone call (what it does, how big it is, etc.)

Preparation for making the phone call

Remember that the person at the other end of the line cannot see you, so you must make the most of your time. Your call has a 'once only' impact for, if you make a hash of it, it is unlikely that you will get another opportunity to put things right.

If you are using a public telephone, choose one which has few distractions (preferably away from a busy shopping area). Always make sure the telephone is in working order and have plenty of correct change.

Before you make the call, write down essential facts about yourself on a small card which will fit in your pocket and be easy to hold in one hand. On the back of this card write prompters for questions about the job and/or company. Have a pen available in case you want to write something such as a telephone number which is best recorded rather than left to memory.

Verbal communication skills

When you are using a telephone in connection with job hunting, you need to take stock of your communication skills. Do you find it easy to communicate? Do others ever have difficulty in understanding you? Do you speak clearly, at a reasonable speed with variation in the tone of your voice? Can you express yourself easily so that there can be an interesting discussion? Do you listen carefully so that you can 'pick up' key responses without any awkward pauses? Have you ever listened to a recording of your voice? Do you sound interested and enthusiastic? Have you ever got anyone to be critical about your telephone manner?

If your answer is always 'YES' then you must be good! If you do not know, perhaps now is the time to find out! If your answer is mainly 'NO' then you have to work on improving your verbal communication skills!

"Hallo, is that Stinton 6020?"
"No, this is Stinton 6220"
"Oh, just a minute —" (checks job advertisement). "Sorry, yes, that's right, can I speak to Mr Robertson?"
"I''ll just see if he's available. Who shall I say is calling?"
"It's about the job vacancy".
"Yes, but who shall I say is calling?"
"Oh, it's Chris — Chris Jones, calling about the job vacancy".
"Thank you. I'm trying to connect you . . . I'm putting you through to Mr Robertson".
"Is that Mr Robertson?"
"Speaking."
"I'm calling about the job vacancy".
"Which vacancy is that?"
"Oh, the one for the sales assistant".
"I see. What is your name, please?"
"I'm sorry — can you hang on a minute? I've dropped my bag".
"I'm holding".
"Yes — well — er . . ."

Listening

How good are your listening skills? Have you ever tried to assess them? There are so many reasons for *not* listening carefully, even when you make a telephone call! For instance, you may be trying to do two things at once, like fumbling for change or pen or paper. You could be distracted by other people trying to get your attention by waving to you or tapping on the call box. There could be extra loud noises of traffic, cars, planes, people shouting or singing.

When telephoning about a job you need to concentrate on what the person at the other end is saying, so that you can develop the conversation into a meaningful discussion.

CHECKLIST 9: USING THE TELEPHONE WHEN JOB HUNTING

1. Find out more about the company: what it does, etc. (get this information from the Jobcentre or local library) ☐

2. KNOW and PLAN beforehand what you are going to say and ask ☐

3. Write down essential facts about yourself, in logical order, on a small card which you can hold in one hand ☐

4. On the back of this card write prompters for questions about the job and company (e.g. pay, hours) ☐

5. Take stock of your communication skills; be aware of areas where you need to take extra care (e.g. shouting down telephone) ☐

6. If you use a public telephone, choose one where you are not likely to have distractions ☐

7. Make sure the telephone is in working order and have plenty of correct change handy ☐

8. Have a pen available to write down important names, numbers, etc. ☐

9. Listen carefully ☐

10. Be BRIEF — CLEAR — PERSUASIVE— try to develop a meaningful discussion ☐

10
Calling at Business Premises

Benefits of the personal visit

It is worth considering whether calling at business premises might suit your style. If you feel more confident about discussing your application in person rather than writing, then this approach should appeal to you and it might be the best way to get that job.

This approach might also be appropriate to your circumstances, your job search area or where you live. For instance, if your job search area includes a concentrated number of employers, as on an industrial estate, it could save you the time and expense that would be involved in writing several letters. On the other hand, your job search area might be bigger and more widespread (say in a rural area) yet it is a small, close community where everyone knows everyone else. In such a situation, you would be expected to apply in person — not by writing.

Another advantage when calling at business premises is that by observing and listening carefully you should be able to get the 'feel' of the place. The way in which people go about their business and the physical aspects of the work situation will reflect the company's policies and procedures, including attitudes towards employees. This should help you decide what it might be like to work for that company.

An added advantage is that this occasion may develop into a **mini-interview.** Even if you don't see the employer, there is always a possibility that someone will pass on to him a few favourable comments about you.

- **What firms** could you visit in your local area?
- Do you know their **addresses?**
- **Transport** — how would you get there?
- **Who** would you ask to see?
- Do you already **know** someone who works there?
- Could someone get you an **introduction?**
- What do you know about these firms' **products** and **services?** Do you have any of their **brochures?**

- What kind of **job** could you see yourself doing there?
- Are they **open** in the daytime, evenings, at weekends?

Making the most of this experience

To make the most of this opportunity, you need to achieve a good impact; therefore you should consider what kind of an impression you are likely to make. The important issues will include

- your appearance
- the way you express yourself
- the extent to which you have prepared for this event and organised information about yourself.

You should aim at creating a good impression so that, when the shortlisting for interview is done, there will be a likeable 'face' to go with your application.

First impressions count

When you are searching for a job, first impressions are most important. You will need to be self-critical about your appearance, making sure you look neat, clean and acceptable. This can be a problem if you decide to call in at several companies during one day, particularly if it involves you in considerable walking or cycling and it is a windy or wet day.

Although it is important to give the right physical impression, you will only make a good impact if you have thought carefully about what is likely to happen, so that you can react naturally and at the same time handle the situation to your advantage. Take with you (for each company you visit) either a typed C.V. or a written record of your name, address, telephone number, age and brief details of your work experience, skills, education and interests. At the bottom of this information, print the names, addresses and telephone number of two people who will give you a reference (try to include the name of someone who knows you in a work situation). Although it will cost you, it might even be worthwhile to include your photograph.

Whom do you hope to see?

Know beforehand what you are going to say when you get inside the business premises, where your first contact is likely to be the receptionist. Be polite and speak clearly. Pay careful attention to non-verbal communication, listen carefully and look interested. Aim at having a realistic attitude and quietly confident manner; be sincere in your intention and hopeful about being given a formal opportunity to present your application.

Be aware of the risks

Calling at business premises can be risky and , if things go wrong, you may just as well write off chances of future employment with that company. You should try to prepare yourself for the unexpected because you never know how the employer or his/her staff will react to you. For instance, you may call at what you think is a reasonable time of the day but you find it is inconvenient and nobody wants to talk to you. Whatever you do in those circumstances, you will be taking a risk, more so if you try to force an interview.

It should help you if you can recognise the danger signals so that you can prevent the situation from worsening and be able to handle things with some sensitivity. For example, if the receptionist has to answer the telephone, what would you do? Thumbs down if you continue to look at her and obviously listen to her conversation! *Thumbs up* if you politely back away, turn round or look elsewhere!

If you want to improve those skills which help you to be sensitive to situations and people you should consider certain points:

- Have you an expressive face? (Sometimes that can land you in trouble and adversely affect your job prospects)
- How good are your observation skills? (Do you always read notices such as 'NO SMOKING'?)
- How perceptive are you about situations and/or people?
- Can you recognise key points in conversation and develop these to your advantage?
- Are you likely to be too 'pushy', or over-confident, or too chatty?

You should think about the different types of situations you might meet when you call at business premises. Aim to be flexible in your approach so that you minimise the risk of things not turning out right for you.

Considering employers' viewpoints

If you decide to call at business premises, you should bear in mind that there are some employers who *insist* on having written letters of application for jobs, whilst others *prefer* written applications and discourage casual callers. However, the majority of employers tend to accept that these days, when jobs are scarce, there will be some people who use their initiative and put a great deal of effort into their job search, including calling at business premises. These are the ones you want to establish contact with. Your local Jobcentre may be able to advise you of some employers' attitudes to casual callers and they should at least be aware of those who insist on written applications. However, for the most part, you have to play this by ear and be prepared for different reactions.

If your approach is planned you are more likely to get a co-operative reaction from the employer or his/her representative. Generally, if an employer thinks that you have taken the trouble to find out about the company, then gone out of your way to visit the place, he/she is likely to consider your application — if only briefly! There could be an advantage to the employer in seeing you without being committed to a full interview. This factor would certainly appeal to someone who regards him/herself as a good judge of people by their appearance and manner, to whom seeing a person is much better than reading a letter of application. Also, there might be a vacancy coming up in the near future and, if an employer thought you suitable, he/she would save a considerable amount of time and money in not having to advertise or pay out interview expenses.

CHECKLIST 10: CALLING AT BUSINESS PREMISES

1. Select this approach if you prefer to discuss your application in person rather than by writing ☐

2. Check with Jobcentre — brief information about employers ☐

3. Be self-critical about your appearance and verbal and non-verbal communication skills ☐

4. Take with you, for each company you visit, C.V. or written personal details ☐

5. Know beforehand what you are going to say — plan to achieve good impact ☐

11
The Employment Interview

Self-assessment

One of the most difficult tasks is to assess oneself objectively. However, as you acquire experience it is usually easier to identify what you are good at and what needs improving upon, possibly by training.

You should start by making a list of **strong points** and **weak points.** When doing this you need to be realistic and honest with yourself, otherwise it becomes a meaningless exercise. You will then be able to identify certain qualities not usually revealed in school reports and certificates obtained. For instance, you may not be academically minded and your exam grades are low; however, you have certain qualities that are more important to some employers than the ability to do well in exams. A sales assistant needs a pleasant personality to encourage customers to return and buy more goods. A job involving repetitive work requires someone with the right kind of temperament — not someone who gets bored by doing the same thing.

Although most adverts require you to write, nowadays an increasing number of employers want you to telephone.

- study the advert carefully,
- think about your strong points in relation to the job,
- then prepare for presentation by letter or telephone.

<u>SELF ASSESSMENT LIST</u> as at April 86

<u>Strong points</u>

Cheerful
Tidy , clean
Sensible -so I'm told
Always on time -punctual
Can be left on my own
    and get on with work
Get on with people
Like working with my hands
Don't mind doing odd jobs

<u>Weak areas</u>

Sometimes impatient
Bad loser
Moody at times
Poor at spelling
    - have to ask
Whistle too much
    at times

How would you assess yourself?

Strong points	Weak areas
_____	_____
_____	_____
_____	_____
_____	_____
_____	_____
_____	_____
_____	_____
_____	_____
_____	_____

Job specification — job description
Most large organisations have formal, written job specifications and it is common to see an advert which invites you to write for application form and further details.

As well as being informative, a job specification enables you to have a very positive approach to the interview because you can study it beforehand and make a note of any query. Then, at the interview, you are more likely to have a meaningful discussion of the job in relation to your suitability. Unfortunately many people just read the job specification and don't bother to use it as a valuable **key to discussion** of their strengths.

If the information about the job is 'in the head' of the interviewer, listen carefully. Get a mental picture of the job and identify the key points.

Typical Job Spec for a Book-keeper

1. Write up Sales Day Book and post entries to Sales Ledger.
2. Write up Purchase Day Book and post entries to Purchase Ledger.
3. Prepare P.A.Y.E. returns.
4. Prepare V.A.T. returns.
5. Draw cheques for wages and salaries.
6. Write up Cash Book and reconcile with weekly bank statements.
7. Write up Petty Cash Book and keep Petty Cash Box.
8. Pay in cash and cheques each day to the Bank.
9. Prepare invoices and monthly statements to customers.
10. Assist the Accounts Manager as required.

Typical Job Spec for an Office Junior

(a) Do all filing for the secretarial pool
(b) Check stationery supplies each week
(c) Fill in departmental job cards each day
(d) Assist with general copy-typing
(e) Assist the Office Manageress
(f) Make tea, run errands and take messages

Interview: expected discussion areas

You should be prepared to discuss any aspect concerning your suitability for the job and adjustment to that particular work situation. Expect to talk about school achievements, work experience, interests and hobbies, relationships with other people and aspects of your home situation which might affect your work.

You may be asked about your hopes and ambitions for the future (difficult to answer unless you have thought about it previously). The interviewer may ask 'What job would you like to be doing in, say 8 years time?' If you are really ambitious, you may think 'Your job!' but don't like to say so for fear of sounding cheeky. You need to think about such questions and decide how you are going to answer them.

Your preparation for the interview

Before the interview you should prepare a **list** of what you want to know about the job and working relationships with the other employees. Job details are usually clearly described but most interviewers rarely comment on **working relationships** unless there are special conditions ('you will have to work closely with . . .'). It is worthwhile considering this aspect and making a note of a few basic questions such as 'How many people will I be working with?', 'What age group are they?'

You also need to think about your appearance and performance at the interview. Your performance will depend on how effectively you communicate with the interviewer, whether or not you are sincere and express yourself clearly and freely. Your appearance should be neat, clean and acceptable.

Interviews — How ready are YOU?

☐ What shall I wear?	☐ Relevant hobbies?
☐ Clean and tidy?	☐ Qualifications?
☐ Feeling fit and well?	☐ Copy of your CV?
☐ A copy of the job ad?	☐ References available?
☐ Knowledge of the work?	☐ When could you start?
☐ Thought about the job?	☐ Pay expectations?
☐ Some questions to ask?	☐ Check time and place?
☐ Clear ambitions?	☐ Know how to get there?
☐ Work experience?	☐ Enough time to get there?

Handling the interview situation

Any interview is partly a science, partly an art! The science part is the extent to which it can be planned and the preparation involved. The art part is the way you handle the interview — cope with the situation.

QUESTIONS YOU MIGHT ASK AT AN INTERVIEW

How many other people would I be working with? What age group are they?

Who will show me what to do?

Would you expect me to wear overalls?

Will I get chance to learn several jobs?

What kind of training will I get? How long will it last? What happens at the end of training?

Will you expect me to continue with education?

What do I need to do to improve my chances of getting this job?

** If there is a formal job description or written details of the job and company, try to relate most of your questions to the information given.

QUESTIONS YOU MIGHT BE ASKED BY THE INTERVIEWER
If a school leaver
What/How do you feel about leaving school? What did you like most about school? What did you achieve? What do you think about your school reference?

General questions
Tell me about yourself (most difficult to answer if you haven't thought about it beforehand). Why do you want this job? (Be honest; not afraid of saying 'I *want work*!') What do you know about us? (Get to know as much as you can about the company beforehand; be prepared to say how you found the information). Have you ever done any part-time work (holidays, weekends, paper rounds, etc)? If so, tell me about it.
How do you get on with other people? Any problems? Have you ever had to deal with any difficult people? What happened? Tell me about the things you do in a typical day. (This could be an important question if you have been out of work for a lengthy period; the employer will want to know if you have done something useful with your time).

What do your parents think about your applying for this job? Do you have to help out at home? If so, what do you have to do? Have you any younger brothers or sisters? If so, do you have to help them?

Are you a practical person? Do you like working with your hands. Any hobbies or interests? How do you feel about . . . overtime? attending college? working on your own? working in a small office? having to stay on at short notice to finish a job? having several junior jobs to do — be at people's beck and call? making tea every morning and afternoon? having to run errands for me? working with several older people?

What do you think about . . . (a current topic which is important either to the company or you or the local community)?

Try to remember that an employment interview is a two-way exchange of information, so it is important for you to let the interviewer know as much as possible about you. In spite of the pressures often associated with an employment interview, try to be natural. There is no point in pretending to be someone else because this will only create a doubt in the mind of the interviewer. If you are yourself, it will help the interview develop into a free-flowing discussion.

The interviewer's assessment of you

An interviewer has to decide whether you can do the job, with training if necessary, and fit in with the other employees. A good interviewer, wanting to be selective, will have an **objective assessment plan** and you will be graded depending on how you match up to the job requirements.

If the **'Five-Fold Plan'** is used, the assessment areas are: Qualifications and Experience; Brains and Innate Abilities; Impact; Motivation; Adjustment. In a large organisation you will probably have to complete selection tests and your potential ability will be assessed for the future.

As well as the employers who use this scientific approach to selection, there are others who rely mainly on their hunches and you may get a job simply because you give the impression of being the right sort of person to do that job (hurrah for the 'vibes' working for you!).

"He had a *very* nice personality. I think he would fit in very well."

"I thought he had a bit of a chip on his shoulder. We'll put a question mark on that one."

"She asked some very good questions, didn't she? I think she'd be very good in dealing with our suppliers."

APPLICANT: David Sedgewick   Seen: 20th June 86

Trainee Tracer (training as draughtsman)

JOB (Requirements)	A	B	Ave C	Poss D	Comments
Age (16)- 18 yrs			✓		
Quals: 'O',CSE gde.1/2 Maths,Eng,Art,etc.				? •	Wait results 3 'O' + 4 CSE (Poor mocks!)
School attendance		✓			
Health		✓			
Eyesight glasses? no colour blind?	✓				Eye test O.K.
Attitude			✓		
Relations with others			✓		Bit offhand
Communication skills			✓		Shy ?
Interests: outdoor indoor		✓	✓		Supports United DIY - models - CB
Work experience			✓		P/T factory in hols

Interviewer's comments: Pleasant - should fit in - if exam results O.K., final interview

Signed: Robert Hope 20.6.86

Selection tests

Many employers wanting more information about applicants will give them selection tests, which may vary from simple mental arithmetic (e.g. 'What is the VAT on . . .?') to comprehensive **aptitude tests** which are used to identify your potential and ability to cope with skills training.

If the job you are interested in involves either specialist or lengthy formal training, you can expect to have to complete a series of tests, both practical and written. These will probably include dexterity tests such as Pin/Peg Board, to test the way and time it is likely to take you to handle work. Then there is the pattern recognition test, where you are required to slot different shaped pieces of wood into their respective positions. Written tests such as the G10 and V10 identify not only your literacy and numeracy but also your intelligence and mechanical aptitude.

PATTERN RECOGNITION

If you have to do such tests, remember it doesn't necessarily depend on how clever you are or how good at writing. Most employers use carefully prepared, often nationally known, practical tests to complete their 'picture' of you, including those aspects which are not covered by your education results, the application or the interview.

If you apply for a job with a large organisation, most probably you will be invited to attend a half-day selection test session, when you and numerous other applicants will have to complete several written and practical tests.

When you have an in-depth interview with your Careers Officer, he/she may ask you to complete DEVAT: several tests that reveal your verbal and numerical reasoning, visual reasoning and mechanical aptitude. In fact, if you receive any vocational guidance counselling, you will have to do several tests so that you can be advised about suitable training to realise your full potential.

If you apply for employment with a company in the food industry, you are required by law to have a thorough medical examination, including X-rays and blood tests. Many other organisations also require you to have some sort of physical test (e.g. for colour-blindness) before confirming your employment.

CHECKLIST 11: THE EMPLOYMENT INTERVIEW

1. Plan and prepare a list beforehand:
   what you will want to know about the job
   and other people in the work situation ☐

2. Consider the kind of questions you might be asked
   and *be prepared to discuss* any aspect of
   your suitability for the job and adjustment
   to the work situation ☐

3. Plan to be punctual for the interview; be
   self-critical about your appearance
   (ask others' advice and comments)
   Look neat, clean and acceptable ☐

4. Expect to be assessed on interview behaviour ☐
   a) Be courteous and polite

   b) Listen carefully ☐

   c) Speak clearly ☐

   d) Establish eye-contact (look at the
      interviewer without 'fixing him')
      Look interested and smile! ☐

   e) Pay careful attention to non-verbal
      communication by being aware of
      mannerisms that might irritate some
      people ☐

   f) Try to establish a mutual exchange of
      comments and discuss freely
      Be natural! ☐

12
Maintaining Your Job Search Programme

Keeping a list of employers and potential employers

If you keep an **updated list** of employers and potential employers, you will be able to keep your finger on the pulse of possible employment. In any event, these days it is wise to have another option and be able to take alternative action — just in case!

If you are unemployed, this list can save you a lot of time and effort. It also means you do not have to rely on Lady Luck — you can use the list in a positive way and plan your job search programme in an organised manner. You don't need to go back to square one just because you aren't successful in getting a job the first time you approach an employer.

Updating your files

It is, of course, most important to keep the details on your list up-to-date so that you can follow up at any time and be aware of possible vacancies arising. So the first thing you need to do to start the list is get, from either the MSC or the main library, the name, address/location, type (manufacture or service) and approximate size of all local companies.

Once you have this basic information, you can add to the list other facts that will further influence your job opportunities. For instance, MSC staff or librarians are likely to comment on some, if not most, of the companies, particularly the MSC who probably have several personal contacts; it is a bonus if you can find out who is responsible for recruitment.

You can add special notes (useful information obtained from hearsay, local papers, advertisements, etc.) and refer to the travel distance and cost involved. In this way you can build up a very helpful **reference file** which will be the basis for your personal job search programme.

- Be organised and systematic
- Keep records so that you can find things quickly
- Try every source of information you can find
- Keep adding information to your collection

PERSONAL JOB SEARCH PROGRAMME

Day/Date/Time	Action	to/person involved	Company concerned	Venue	Job vacancy/result	Follow-up/comments
MON 2 JUN	Letter	C. Moore Personal Officer	Excell Ltd Park Road DURHAM D10 2L		Accept offer to be put on their waiting list	Note of future 5 star company
TUE 3 JUN 9.30am	Interview Selection Tests	Report to Training Officer	Easi-Fit Ltd Industrial Estate	Training Centre	Trainee Computer Operator	Doubtful – 10 on shortlist
THU 5 JUN 2.30pm	Interview	T. Norton	Norton, Bile & Boff Solicitors Winsley Road	Office	YTS Junior Clerical Assistant	C.O. arranged – should be offered this. – might I accept – not sure would like job + YTS!! Action after interview, phone C.O.
FRI 6 JUN	Phone (30261)	Career Officer				

TUE Jobcentre a.m. Library p.m.
WED See/phone Career Jobcentre p.m. ?
THU Library - local paper ads/vacs ?
FRI Action any poss job - telephone, write, call in

Keeping a record of those employers who have your name on their Waiting List

If you are ever asked whether you wish to have your name kept on a waiting list, say 'Yes, please!' and be prepared to follow up this sign of approval that you are worthwhile being considered for employment with that company.

Please do not assume that you should then sit back and wait for them to contact you. It is up to you to use this experience in a positive and, hopefully, eventually successful way by

- making a brief record of the company's rating as an employer
- following up in a planned approach.

In this way you sustain the company's interest in you by letting them know about your keenness to work for them.

Aim at a simple yet clear record. Note any special details including employee benefits such as free protective clothing/equipment; cheap 'seconds'; training; opportunities for advancement. Avoid recording only details which might change, when there are other essential facts. For instance, 'X' company pays £20 per week more than other employers; travel may well involve cost of £18 per week.

It is best to keep your record brief, either on the back of the company's letter (invitation to interview, etc.) or on a card. Whichever method of reference you choose, it is advisable to keep the information in a file marked **Employers Waiting List** or something similar.

The important thing is to have a brief, clear reference which can be updated and used in your job search. Thus, if you haven't heard from such an employer for several months, you can approach the company and remind them, in the nicest way, that you are still keen to join the organisation. Usually such positive action yields success!

Name of Firm: _____

Address: _____

Phone No: _____

Personal Contact: _____

Job applied for: _____

Approx. rates of pay: _____

Training opportunities: _____

Notes: _____

Establishing your personal job search programme

Once you have compiled a list of employers, it will be possible to decide a plan of action and initiate your personal job search programme. This needs to be organised in advance, as a **weekly diary,** indicating basic information such as time of interview, place, company, together with other relevant details (4-star company; good prospects; job sounds great, etc).

Initially it can be fairly simple, comparable to a working diary where the aim is accuracy concerning time, date, venue, name of person or company involved. However, in areas of high unemployment this plan needs to include other influencing factors. For instance, if local newspaper headlines are 'X Company redundancies!' the employment chances are unlikely to be good. If, however, the headlines are 'X Company — additional investment of £3m!' then there should be good employment prospects.

Reviewing progress

To use your experience and make your efforts worthwhile, you should look critically at your personal job search programme at the end of each week and every month to see how you are progressing.

At its best, this action plan can be developed into an organised and meaningful job search programme. Furthermore, it is good thinking to use such a plan because it encourages you to organise your time in a constructive way. Also, your concentrated efforts are likely to result in the most successful approach towards job hunting.

Developing your plan of action

If you want to intensify your job search, it will inevitably involve consideration of several 'possible' jobs at the same time. This might worry you. You might even find yourself in a position where you feel uneasy and doubtful about discussing other pending interviews; consequently your comments are likely to be vague, even evasive.

You need to be aware of such pitfalls when developing your plan of action. From your point of view, you are being realistic *and* modest by not assuming you will get that particular job. Also, if you wait and apply for one vacancy at a time, you may well be missing out on a more suitable job whilst your application is being processed. This could be very time-consuming if there are a few hundred applications to be sorted.

The sensible approach

Prospective employers will realise that it is not easy to get a job these days, so that if you are keen to work you *must* follow up several vacancies at once. Most employers do not lose interest when they find out that other interviews are 'in the pipeline', provided you are honest and sincere in your intentions.

However, beware of being tempted to use other interviews as a bargaining ploy to force an offer of employment. The other sensitive situation is if you are awaiting results of another interview. In either instance, there is a need for planning beforehand what your approach is going to be, bearing in mind that the effective employment interview should reflect a situation where there is frank and open discussion between you and your prospective boss.

CHECKLIST 12: KEEPING CONTACT WITH EMPLOYMENT SOURCES AND DEVELOPING YOUR OWN JOB SEARCH PROGRAMME

1.   Prepare a list of employers and potential employers ☐
        Get basic details of these from MSC or main library ☐
        Add other facts which will influence job opportunities with these firms ☐
        Keep details up-to-date ☐

2.   Prepare a record of those employers who have your name on their Waiting List ☐
        Keep a file 'Employers Waiting List' ☐
        Brief, clear reference which can be updated and used in job search ☐
        Use to follow up and remind those employers that you are still interested in employment with them ☐

3.   Establish your personal job search programme — plan of action ☐
        Organise in advance a weekly working diary showing time, date, venue, name of person and company involved and other special notes/influencing factors ☐
        Prepare an organised and meaningful job search programme ☐

4.   Develop your plan of action ☐
        Plan job search — several jobs at one time ☐
        Show you are keen to work — be open about following up several jobs at once ☐
        Be honest and sincere about your intentions ☐
        Plan approach beforehand ☐
        Aim at effective employment interview — frank and open discussion ☐

13
Getting Practice and Help

Although practice doesn't always make you perfect, it *does* get you used to situations. It also helps you develop your job search skills.

Letter writing
This is an occasion when you have to determine clearly what you aim to get out of the exercise. Also, those who help must try to ignore the fact that you are the writer. They should react naturally and instinctively, as if they had received the letter from someone unknown.

All concerned should agree that the essentials of a good letter of application will include:

- legible handwriting
- correct spelling
- appropriate punctuation
- style reflecting you as an individual
- courtesy, including prompt reply to company letter
- good business format
- balanced paragraphs

You need to PRACTISE and your family and friends need to REACT instinctively — they should not take time in reaching conclusions.

PRACTISE *describing your strong points without seeming big-headed*
Example: My references will confirm that I am a good timekeeper and conscientious at work.

PRACTISE *getting over the right message*
Example: Given the opportunity, I intend working hard because I *want* to do this kind of job.

In short, you need to PRACTISE *communicating your personal characteristics and abilities honestly and sincerely, emphasising your strong points without sounding too full of your own importance.*

AIM to get the appropriate impact on paper!

Employment interview situations

This is a sensitive area and calls for considerable thought about the people who are involved and what is going to be achieved. It is best to get friends rather than family to help because it is usually difficult for relatives to be impartial. On the other hand members of the family, particularly parents, are likely to be more experienced and aware of the pitfalls.

How many helpers?

It is usually most helpful if there are only two people because even a small group can get too chatty, so that it becomes difficult to exercise self-control and keep quiet. Additionally, if there are only two people involved, the 'one-to-one' discussion is more likely to be realistic. If you are a nervous, shy or quiet person, you should get much more out of this experience and it is bound to help you when it comes to the real interview.

Of course there *are* advantages in having a few observers and listeners because these people could make some useful comments. It really depends on the people concerned and how committed they are to helping you and being constructive in what they say. Usually, unless a group situation is controlled by someone experienced in such **role play** situations, it is more likely that negative comments will be made about the interviewee's (your) performance. Also you are less likely to be natural because you will be aware of those watchers and feel self-conscious about everything you do and say.

Whatever is decided about the number of people taking part, it is essential that:

- you establish beforehand what the interview situation is so that the purpose may be clearly identified

- your interviewer prepares some sort of plan: decides on a few questions and what areas are to be discussed (he/she should aim to cover only a few points)

- you (as interviewee) have a plan; aim at referring to your strong points and be prepared for discussion of relevant areas

If possible, **tape the interview.** No-one can argue with a recording of what is said. It will also ensure that you can have a rational discussion about the areas to be improved upon.

The overall aim should be that your practice employment interview is meaningful and worthwhile. At worst, this sensitive situation could end a good friendship because you do not see eye-to-eye about certain points. At best, you could both learn from the experience and develop the skills necessary for an effective interview.

Using the telephone when job hunting — taped discussions, role play
Although a beneficial exercise for would-be telephone job searchers, this can become a fun area that rapidly gets out of hand and is regarded as a big joke. If you *do* decide to practise using the telephone, you and anyone involved must be prepared to concentrate and imagine it is a 'for real' phone-in.

Bearing this in mind, you need a typical situation so that the person who 'answers' your telephone call knows whom he/she represents and can discuss the job details. Therefore each of you must have a copy of the information concerning the company and the job, so that it will be realistic.

Organise yourself
Before you start, you need to organise your efforts and consider the following:

- The **physical arrangement** is important as the usual family situation makes it necessary for both of you to be in the same room. It may even involve special arrangements to get a room to yourselves. However, you must *not* be able to see each other whilst you are talking, so — back to back, and *no cheating*!

- Ensure that the **tape recorder** is working efficiently. If you find at the end of the conversation that it wasn't working, hard luck! Make sure it is switched on to record the conversation.

- **Record** the complete conversation.

- Before you play back, have a **brief discussion** and try to be constructively critical about each other's performance, even though more importance is attached to the job seeker's performance.

- Have pen and paper handy to make **notes** during the playback.

- **Play back:** listen to the complete record of the conversation (*DO NOT STOP TAPE*)

- Note main areas needing **improvement,** such as hesitation, not clear, etc.

- After playback, **compare notes and discuss** the complete situation, referring to specific parts of the conversation.

Perhaps this is an occasion when you might coax some of the family to help you. It would certainly be useful if more experienced people could be persuaded to take part, if only in a general discussion. However, no matter who is involved, this is an area where you always learn something about your telephone technique and manner of communicating. It is well worth doing!

CHECKLIST 13: PRACTISING WITH HELP OF FRIENDS AND FAMILY

1.   **Letter writing** ☐
        Practise the essentials of writing a good business letter: legible writing; correct spelling; appropriate punctuation; good business format; balanced paragraphs ☐
        Practise writing about yourself: describing your strong points, getting over the right message in a brief, sincere way ☐

2.   **Employment interview situations** ☐
        Have only two people involved: you, being interviewed, and another as interviewer ☐
        One-to-one discussion; each has an interview plan, according to role ☐
        Tackle only a few discussion areas ☐
        Preferably tape the discussion ☐
        Aim to have a practice interview which is meaningful and worthwhile, so that you will both learn from the experience and develop the skills necessary for an employment interview situation ☐

3.   **Using telephone when job hunting — taped discussion, role play** ☐
        Clearly establish the role play situation, each having written details of the company and the job ☐
        Organise your efforts: prepare room, back-to-back, tape recorder in good working order ☐
        Concentrate: imagine it is a 'for-real' phone-in situation ☐
        Record the complete conversation. Briefly discuss before playback ☐
        Play back *all* **the taped discussion; LISTEN and make notes, if necessary** ☐
        Afterwards, compare notes and discuss the complete situation; refer to tape ☐

14
Making Good Use of your Time

Develop your skills

Frequently it is that additional skill which is the deciding factor in getting the job, so it is to your advantage if you use your time constructively.

Some of the possibilities are obvious. For instance, if you are interested in getting a full-time clerical job, you need to find out the best, quickest and least costly way of acquiring skills associated with working in an office. You can attend a college to get **typing and keyboard skills** (if you are under 18 years old it won't cost anything at a College of Further Education). Several organisations offer short, intensive courses so you can acquire skills within minimum time, at a price. The best approach is to find out what facilities are available, through your Jobcentre or local library.

Your driving licence

The ability to drive is a practical skill which is most useful when searching for a job, as well as being highly desirable for personal reasons. You may not have passed your driving test but if you are able to write down that you have a provisional driving licence it reflects your ambitions/ intentions and gives you an advantage over someone who hasn't bothered.

First aid

One skill which tends to be thought of as an interest rather than being related to work concerns First Aid. If you are a qualified First Aider, trained in St. John Ambulance work, it would undoubtedly have a great influence on your getting a job. Do not forget that all firms need to be covered for Health and Safety regulations.

Correspondence courses

nother consideration is whether to take a correspondence course. Nowadays there are reputable organisations such as the International Correspondence School and the Business Correspondence School which offer several correspondence courses leading to recognised examinations.

Obviously a correspondence course favours the kind of skills which involve writing, including accountancy, ranging from G.C.E. 'O' levels and languages to professional qualifications (in which case studies are related to the respective professional institute).

Skills training

Some national organisations offer skills training. Typical examples would include the Territorial Army, R.A.F. Cadets, Naval Cadets, Sea Scouts and Rangers as well as organised Youth Club activities (working for the Duke of Edinburgh's Awards).

Gaining experience

Then there are the skills which you can develop indirectly as a result of experience. A good example of this is doing **voluntary work** with local voluntary organisations. It is surprising how much information and expertise you can acquire in, say, organising and administration, social skills, getting on with different types of people or manual skills such as helping to decorate for old people. You may not be trained to do the job but you pick up the skill by watching other people do it, then you have a go yourself!

Keep fit for work

Many unemployed people don't realise they need to keep fit for work. It is so very easy to get unfit! If you are unemployed and keep getting rejected for jobs, it seems natural to stay in bed in the morning, thinking 'What have I got to get up for?' (isn't it snug to turn over and say that on a cold morning!). Well, when you do that, probably someone shouts at you to get up, and it's not just because that someone thinks it will be good for you not to develop idle habits (although of course that is true!). It's because someone knows that young people need to be into physical things — action!!

It is not suggested that you become a sports fanatic or athlete, although these would involve getting very fit and at the same time provide most absorbing interests. However, you *do* need to be realistic and ask youself how fit are you? Most of all, can you complete a hard day's work (even in a job not reckoned to be physical) and keep up a good performance for the rest of the week.

In some jobs, the demand for a certain standard of fitness can be exhausting. Those jobs are obviously physical — labouring, manual work, etc. However, every job demands a certain fitness, even though at first this may not be apparent. For instance, a sales assistant is able to move about the shop but has to stand all day. A factory machinist has to sit on the same seat, in the same place, with the same body movements, to do his/her job each day at work.

When a potential employer assesses you, he/she is likely to rate this fitness factor fairly high. If you turn up for the interview looking pale, with 'bags' under your eyes, giving a general impression of being tired out, it is not surprising if there is a big question mark at the side of 'fitness rating'. In such circumstances, the typical question would be 'What do you do with yourself all day?'

Don't let your body get used to staying in bed until 10 or 11 a.m., then phasing out the day to make it last. Make good use of your time; have a healthy attitude towards keeping fit for work!

Passport to Leisure!

If you live within a city area or a place where there is high unemployment, it is advisable to find out from your local library or Recreation Centre whether or not there is a scheme operating whereby, as an unemployed young person, you may enjoy leisure facilities such as swimming, snooker, badminton, table-tennis — *free of charge!*

Some cities have excellent schemes to help in this way. Sheffield is one example. It encourages the unemployed to keep fit in mind and body — hopefully for work! Sheffield offers a 'Passport to Leisure'!

This concession is only available for people who live within the city boundary. The Recreation Department produces a series of leaflets which cover different leisure activities (e.g. swimming and sports centre facilities) with useful explanatory notes on how to apply. When you are accepted you get your 'Passport to Leisure' (a pass which includes your photograph) and become eligible to use all the facilities either free of charge or for a small cost.

Know your support services

All too frequently, young people find out about government benefits and local supportive facilities as a last resort, by which time they may have unnecessarily experienced strained circumstances.

The extent to which young people *know* about available financial aid tends to vary considerably, depending on whether they live in a rural or city area and on other people who are involved in preparation for leaving school and starting work. Occasionally newspapers inform about important issues such as 'Claiming Benefits' but generally this kind of information is communicated by teachers, Careers Officers, Youth Clubs and, of course, parents. You may be lucky in getting to know about the various ways in which help is available, including explanatory leaflets. However, it may well be a case of 'If you don't ask, you won't get . . .', so you need to have some idea of where to go for information.

Using the DHSS

If you want information about financial benefits, you should visit your local DHSS where the staff should be able to advise and help, particularly if you have a special problem. They will put you in touch with the appropriate community service (e.g. Social Services). They also issue free pamphlets which explain clearly what is involved in such important matters as claiming state benefits whilst unemployed, supplementary benefit, etc. These pamphlets are published and updated by the **Central Office of Information** (C.O.I.) — very necessary nowadays because of changing government regulations.

Citizens Advice Bureaux

Another source of help is the Citizens Advice Bureau, where you may get free and impartial advice about a wide variety of issues including personal welfare, legal aid and financial problems. The C.A.B. also supply informative leaflets (same as the DHSS) as well as advising you how to go about things. They can put you in touch with other organisations (such as the DHSS) including private local organisations and charities which are prepared to assist young people.

The important thing here is to know what assistance is available and how to go about getting help when it is needed.

> Decide what to do,
> to learn something new;
> Keep busy, keep fit
> — then you won't feel so blue
> Make leisure a pleasure
> Till that job is in view!

15
Working Abroad

Personal considerations

Working abroad not only involves considering legal requirements, there are also personal issues which are particularly important if your contract covers 2 years or more.

Although your contract will refer to pay, you will need to bear in mind those other factors which have a considerable influence on your money. For example, if the **cost of living** is extraordinarily high (as it is in some European countries) you will find it difficult to save and, even if you do save, there may be problems in transferring your savings back home. Other influences on your money will be rate of exchange and tax regulations.

Spending and saving

You will want to estimate how much you are likely to spend on **accommodation and food,** even though your contract states that these are provided free. Your estimate will presumably reflect your intended life-style. For instance, if you are highly motivated to save, then you will be prepared to exist on whatever is provided free of charge; on the other hand, you may like your extra comforts, in which case you will need to be prepared to pay for these. Similarly with **leisure** pursuits, which may also involve legal restrictions (e.g. banning of alcohol in many Middle Eastern countries).

Insurance

Another issue in your contract will concern insurance. Although your employer will advise on this, it is as well to check every aspect in relation to your particular needs because people have different ideas about the extent to which they should be insured. Obviously a lot depends on the country and work situation (some countries, such as Australia, require you to have health insurance). If in doubt, it is advisable to contact one of the specialist insurance companies.

You also need to bear in mind that your position could quickly be affected by changes in the **political** scene.

Employment opportunities in E.E.C. countries

The big advantage about working in one of the E.E.C. countries is that there is legally free movement of labour, therefore you don't need a work permit. However, you *do* have to **register** with the local authorities concerned in order to get a **residence permit.** Usually this involves supplying some written evidence to confirm that you have been offered at least three months' employment.

It is a good idea to contact your Jobcentre because occasionally they have details of vacancies in E.E.C. countries. You can also obtain from them a useful leaflet, *Working Abroad,* which tells you how to get a job abroad and what kind of things you need to consider before accepting employment.

Additionally, they should be able to supply you with names and addresses of agencies and British firms that have branches in E.E.C. countries. If you decide to write to these contacts, it is advisable to include an International Reply Coupon (obtainable from Post Offices), your C.V. and comprehensive details of what you can offer, as well as the type of work you are seeking. Should you use the services of an employment agency abroad, remember that you and your prospective employer will be charged a fee for this service.

Short-term work opportunities

There are likely to be more opportunities for short-term employment, particularly seasonal or summer vacation work in industries such as catering, hotels, etc. Some organisations arrange employment on an exchange basis; for instance, the British Hotels, Restaurants and Caterers Association runs international schemes, on a quota basis, for young people in the catering industry. It is possible to find work, usually as a junior commis waiter/waitress, for periods of up to one year in most European countries.

You could also reply to adverts in British or foreign newspapers or trade journals. However, as it is easy to travel in E.E.C. countries, you may decide to do so and try to get work 'on spec'. If you do this, you should be prepared for problems such as poor pay, uninteresting and hard manual work, difficulties in finding accommodation, considerable travel and expense in getting to work.

Whichever way you choose to carry out your job search, remember that if unemployment increases in your chosen country, it will be much more difficult to get any type of work!

Employment opportunities in countries other than the E.E.C.

If you are interested in working abroad for a lengthy period, you should first of all contact the foreign Embassy concerned, who will advise you on the existing situation and relevant regulations.

Regulations concerning work and residence permits differ from country to country but basically they depend on:

- having a positive job offer
- being able to speak the language
- having pre-arranged accommodation.

Usually your prospective employer will have to apply for your **work permit.** In Third World countries each company is granted permits on a **quota** basis and, as the rules are strictly enforced, you are only likely to be accepted for a specified time of 2-3 years. In Australia, it would be 3-5 years. Religious organisations usually require a minimum contract of 2 years; also, if you wish to be considered for such employment, you not only have to practise your religion but you will be expected to have a degree, professional qualification or practical skills.

You stand a better chance of getting a work permit if you are interested in a *temporary job* or a *working holiday*. In that case, the Embassy concerned will be able to advise you whom you should contact. You can also obtain useful details from publications such as: *Directory of Summer Jobs Abroad* (published by Vacation Work) *Summer Employment Directory of the U.S.* (published by Vacation Work) *Working Holidays* (Central Bureau for Educational Visits and Exchanges).

Then there are voluntary organisations such as TOC H Clayton Volunteers (various programmes in the U.S.A.). Also, you might qualify for being considered on an exchange basis for a specified period. Although this type of scheme favours professional people or undergraduates (as part of their educational studies) there is an increasing tendency for other organisations, including Youth Services and Trade Unions, to include this experience as part of their training programme.

Other useful **How To . . . Books:**

How to Get a Job Abroad Alan Jones
A unique guide to landing thosed hard-to-get assignments overseas.
0 7463 0325 4

How to Live & Work in Australia Laura Veltman
An essential handbook for all those considering employment and residence "Down Under". 0 7463 0331 9

How to Live & Work in America Steve Mills
Expert advice for everyone contemplating Stateside employment and residence. 0 7463 0330 0

Northcote House Publishers Ltd., Harper & Row House, Estover Road, Plymouth PL6 7PZ, United Kingdom. Tel: Plymouth (0752) 705251. Telex: 45635.

Voluntary work overseas

If you are unemployed, independent, have some skills and wish to gain experience which should eventually help you get a good job, then you could consider working abroad for a voluntary organisation. Generally you should be over 18 years old (some organisations such as V.S.O. specify age over 20 years); however there are a few programmes which have a minimum age of 17 years.

Although there are more opportunities to work in Third World countries such as Africa, Asia and Latin America, there is a need for volunteers in more developed parts of the world. In such countries invaluable work is done by volunteers representing many well-known national and international voluntary organisations, both religious and non-religious. Some of these are run privately, others partly funded by governments.

Most of these organisations regularly publicise work opportunities in leaflets and notices which give details of the country involved, age range and skills required and minimum duration of contract to be served. As a volunteer you would be regarded as an unpaid worker, entitled to free food and accommodation as well as a regular 'allowance' which, in many instances, would be more than local pay.

If you are interested in doing voluntary work abroad, you can obtain names and addresses of relevant organisations from your Careers Office, Jobcentre or main library. Rather than write to the organisation concerned, it may be possible to telephone and find out more information from a local representative.

In most areas the Careers Service regularly produces informative leaflets on voluntary work overseas. These refer to useful publications and give addresses. These are just a few:

- 'The International Directory of Voluntary Work': pub. Vacation Work

- 'Kibbutz Volunteer': pub. Vacation Work

- 'British Volunteer Programme': 22 Coleman Fields, London N1

More importantly, there are details of organisations and specific work areas where volunteers are needed; such as:

- World Community Development Service (Junior Volunteer Schemes) 27 Montague Road, Botley, Oxford OX2 9AH. Minimum age 17½ yrs. 6 months — 1 year. India, Kenya, Sri Lanka. No academic qualifications required.

- Missions to Seamen
  St. Michael Paternoster Royal, College Hill, London EC4R 2RL

Minimum age 18. Europe, Far East, Australia. Communicant Anglicans, able to swim, with valid driving licence. Minimum 6 months service.

You are likely to be interested in voluntary work overseas if you want to commit yourself for a specified time to helping in a particular programme. The main thing is to ensure you really want to do such work so that, although the money side is insignificant, you will achieve considerable satisfaction from doing a worthwhile job helping others.

Working holidays abroad

As there are currently 30,000 (mainly E.E.C.) vacation jobs available, this is an important area for your job search!

Nowadays there are many opportunities to earn money by working at the same time as being on holiday abroad. Although most young people who take advantage of this situation are students on Higher Education courses, these opportunities are open to any unemployed 18-25 year old. Most probably students on Higher Education courses are involved because they *know* about such opportunities! Vacation is the only time they can earn money and let's face it, despite educational grants, most young people want to have money in their pockets to buy those other things that make life enjoyable. Also, they are encouraged to have a change from the academic life and what better way than to take a working holiday? Furthermore, reputable leisure organisations such as PGL go out of their way to encourage applications from such students; consequently there is a mass of information displayed in the college/university library. So, if you fit into this category, as a student/undergraduate on a Higher Education course, you won't have to search for an address to write to or a form to complete. Just pop into the library!

If, however, you are the average unemployed 18-25 year old who does not often visit main libraries, it is unlikely that you will see such inviting literature. Of course, you may happen to hear a radio programme about working holidays, in which case you will know how to go about things.

Generally, though, if you *are* interested, you will need to go to a main library to discover in detail what you have to do. You will find there are some good reference books which explain whom to contact. This will involve writing a letter of application, together with your C.V. and possibly a photograph (some organisations may require this). If your initial approach is satisfactory, you will be asked to complete an application form. In some instances the application form may consist of several sheets.

The type of organisation that offers such holiday employment varies from small firms to large international companies. Some offer first-class training as well as pay, accommodation and food but obviously the 'package' will vary. For example, the pay may be low but the standard of food and accommodation high. Or you may have to accept some discomfort but remember that you are being paid and that, furthermore, you will acquire certain skills and experience which may help you get a permanent job!

CHECKLIST 15: WORKING ABROAD

1. If you intend working in a country
   which is not in the E.E.C.,
   first contact the Embassy concerned ☐

2. Make sure you fully understand your employment
   contract particularly legal implications
   and insurance aspects ☐

3. Find out as much as possible about living
   conditions — climate, accommodation, etc ☐

16
Ethnic Minorities

You should take full advantage of the support facilities available from your particular ethnic group! You may belong to one of the bigger, well-established and more traditional ethnic groups, in which case your life will already be organised in a distinctive way. Or your immediate family may be self-sufficient and run its own business. Either way, you will be able to benefit from the educational and training facilities available to everyone living in Britain.

Community groups
If necessary, you can widen your contacts through your local **Community Relations Council,** which represents local ethnic groups as well as a wide range of other organisations — leisure groups, the Red Cross, religious groups, etc. Also, you may be lucky enough to be in an area where there are special organisations set up to deal with specific problems such as unemployment. You will be able to get these names and addresses from your local telephone directory. The main thing is for you to find out what facilities are available and how you can benefit from them.

Presenting yourself
Without the backing of a community group it will be that much more necessary to follow the advice given in this book. You will notice that one of the main issues concerns presenting yourself in the best possible way. Probably your most effective way to be considered for employment is a 'planned' call at selected business premises. If you take the trouble to plan, as advised in Chapter 10, you will be able to discuss your strengths in relation to the job/work situation and the employer will tend to consider you on your true merits.

It will also be important to remember differences in customs can be misinterpreted. For instance, a modest, downcast look could be thought of as being 'shifty' or evasive. The custom of avoiding eye-contact with a stranger may be regarded as indifference. You have only to think of the different forms of greeting all around the world, including kissing on both cheeks and rubbing noses, and you soon realise that there are many ways of getting the message across.

What *you* have to do is decide beforehand what is likely to be acceptable in your situation. If you are thorough in your approach and think about it carefully, then hopefully, you will be able to present yourself in the best possible way and make the necessary impact to get that job!

17
Sample Letters

Good letters are perhaps more vital in job-hunting than in any other aspect of daily life. The following pages contain a set of sample letters to cover a range of needs. Try not to follow them slavishly! — develop and refine your own to meet your own specific needs.

- Don't just send off your first draft
- Read it through and re-draft if necessary
- Ask a friend or relative for their comments before you send it off

When looking at the sample letters shown on the next pages, be **critical.** Get practice in asking yourself these questions, about your own letters:
- ☐ Is it addressed to the right person?
- ☐ Is it properly laid out (good format) and dated?
- ☐ Does it stick to the point?
- ☐ Does it sound business-like and natural?
- ☐ Have I made the main points I wanted to?
- ☐ Does it sound confident and positive?
- ☐ Is the handwriting really clear?
- ☐ Is the signature legible, or if not have I printed my name underneath?

And before you rush off to the letterbox with it:

- ☐ Have I got someone else to read through it?
- ☐ Did I remember all the enclosures?
- ☐ Do I need to keep a copy of the letter, and of any enclosures?
- ☐ Should I enclose a stamped self-addressed envelope?
- ☐ Should it go first class?

Good luck!

EXPLORATORY LETTER

83 York Road,
Bilsden,
Yorkshire
BY2 9NP

Telephone: Bilsden 12045

Dear Sir,
20th Mar 86

I am 16 yrs old and left Bilsden Comprehensive last July. I passed C.S.E.s in English, Maths, Woodwork and Technical Drawing which is my best subject.

Next week I complete a YTS course where I've worked for the Council and gone to the local Tech for Block Release. There is no chance of a job with them so I thought I'd write off to a few employers.

I am good with my hands, don't mind hard work and am quite strong. I help my dad quite a lot at home. My supervisor will give me a good reference about my work and timekeeping.

Will you please consider me for a job. I should be grateful if you could interview me.

Yours truly,

Tim White

Manager,
Tripot PLC,
Industrial Estate,
Bilsden
Yorkshire BY1 LPZ

Comments reflect a good profile with a natural style. However, it is not as informative as it should be concerning the length of the YTS course, skills acquired and job/work experience details. A typed C.V. would complement this letter and create the necessary impact.

EXPLORATORY LETTER

Tel: Birley 89643

4 Tower Road
Birley
Lancs BL3 9FM

21st April 1986

Dear Mr Lloyd,

As your company usually takes on a few college leavers each year, I thought I would write and enquire whether you are likely to have a suitable vacancy for me.

At present I am on a 2yr Business Studies (BTEC) National Diploma Course which finishes in June this year. If possible, I want to get a job involving computers as I am interested in this field and consider that I can offer some experience.

I attach my C.V. and meanwhile would welcome the opportunity to discuss my career prospects with your organisation.

Yours sincerely
Jane Frodsham

Mr J Lloyd,
Personnel Manager
International Chemicals Ltd,
Birley
BL1 6AR

Has made good use of her knowledge of the company (found out the name of the Personnel Manager etc.). The letter is also persuasive — it would complement her typed C.V. and be likely to get the reader to think seriously about seeing her.

REPLY TO ADVERT WHICH ASKED APPLICANTS TO WRITE FOR FURTHER DETAILS AND APPLICATION FORM

REF: JUNIOR ASSISTANT

20 Wogan Road
Mapperly
Nr Dirby
D1J 4TV

Telephone : Dirby 50132

Dear Mr Wood,   5th May 1986

I wish to apply for the above job advertised in today's Guardian. I left school at Christmas and am doing a Community Programme which is due to finish next month. What I am doing is mainly outside work — gardening and sweeping — but I am used to answering the phone and would like to do Office work. At present I work for the Council who will give me good references.

Will you please send me further details and an application form which I will complete straight away. Thank you.

Adam Blissett

Mr K. Wood
Manager
Bee Bright Ltd
Main Elm Road
Dirby
D40 AN

Prompt reply. Included some useful information about himself (implied flexibility and direct keenness). Natural 'tone'.

REPLY TO ADVERT

12 Navigation Road (bud)
Puddlewich
Nr. Stafford
Staffordshire PQ1 30S

Ref: Office Junior

Telephone Puddlewich 5812

20th March 1986

Dear Mr. Pears

I wish to apply for the above-mentioned position.
I am 17 years old, with 'O' level English Language
and 5 C.S.Es including Maths and Commerce.
At present I am attending a 1yr. Business
Studies Course at the local College of Further
Education. This course finishes in June when I
shall be taking BEC exams in People & Communication,
World of Work, Business Calculations, Data
Processing and R.S.A. Typing Stage II.
Your firm has a good reputation for training young
people and if I am given the opportunity, I intend
to work hard and improve my office skills -
particularly typing. The job also appeals to me
because it is in a small, busy office (I think
I would enjoy that!)
I attach my C.V. and hope to hear from you.

Yours sincerely,

Margaret Pagden

Mr K N Pears
Solicitor
Merrydown Road
Stafford
SL4 1PG

Good immediate impact, although the 1st paragraph is too lengthy — it
seems to be *too* carefully written. The 2nd paragraph is most impressive
— reflects her enthusiasm, attitude, aims etc. Should get the writer an
interview!

REPLY TO ADVERT

Ref: Vacancy
Trainee VDU Operator.

12 Park Lane,
Crispen.
Nr Alton.
A21 CY34

Telephone: Alton 70132

Dear Mr Browne,   4th Jun 86

I wish to apply for the above post which was advertised in yesterday's Chronicle.

I am 18 years old and have 'O' levels in English + Maths as well as 5 C.S.E.s including Technical Drawing and Geography.

Since leaving Carlton Comprehensive I have worked relief at Bungos Warehouse and done general office work for C.E. Cotes Electrical. However, I am keen to get a permanent job.

Your vacancy interests me because I should get training in something I like dealing with — computers. Also your company has got a good reputation and if I am given the opportunity I shall work hard.

I am available for interview at any time. If you phone Mr Elliot at Bungos (Alton 5412) and Mr Cotes (Alton 9824) they will give me a good reference.

Yours sincerely
Peter Martin

Mr N. Browne
Personnel Manager
A.C.S. Ltd
Alton A34 2IN

Contents of the letter are informative and well organised, giving a clear profile of Peter. He has written about his strong points in relation to job details (advert also stated preference for 'O' level English and Maths); also given reference phone numbers.

REPLY TO LETTER REQUESTING INTERVIEW AND CERTIFICATES

Your ref: NB/As/Vac

12 Park Lane
Crispen
Nr Alton A21 CY34

Telephone: Alton 70132

8th Jun 86

Dear Mr Browne,

Thank you for your letter dated 7th Jun inviting me to attend interview on Thursday 11th Jun at 9.30 a.m. for Selection testing.

I understand that it will take all morning and will be pleased to bring my certificates with me when I report to the Training Centre.

Thank you for giving me this opportunity.

Yours sincerely,

Peter Martin

Mr N. Browne
Personnel Manager
A.C.S. Ltd
Alton A34 2IN

Prompt reply — brief and clear confirmation. Has copied the business format indicated in the company's letter.

ACKNOWLEDGEMENT OF LETTER REQUESTING INTERVIEW

Tel : Bestwick 48120

2 Marton Lane
Gawsworth
Nr Bestwick
BK1 3QA

19th June 86

Dear Mrs Brand

Thank you for your letter dated 17th June. I shall be pleased to attend interview on Wednesday 25th June at 10.45 a.m. and will bring my driving licence and copy of my college report. I look forward to seeing you.

Yours sincerely

Allan Stuart

Mrs T. Brand
Staff Manageress
Super-Buy Stores
Bestwick
BK 2P9

Prompt — brief — clear!

ACKNOWLEDGEMENT OF REJECTION LETTER AND, AT SAME TIME, REQUEST TO BE PUT ON WAITING LIST

20 Maple Avenue
Bolingbrook
Newton

NB 2 CH

Mr S. Sparkes
Manager
Magnetic Plc.
Barnes Road
Newton N3 4DJ

21st April 86

Dear Mr Sparkes,

Thank you for your letter dated 16 th April. Although disappointed by not being chosen, I was pleased to be short-listed and enjoyed my tour of your factory. I wonder if I can ask you to consider keeping my application on a Waiting List for future employment.

I am not sure if you keep such a list but, if so, I would be most grateful to be considered when you have another vacancy. I really would like to work for your company.

Yours sincerely,
Betty Feather

Polite acknowledgement. Request shows keenness to work for company — more important, it can be followed up when there *is* a vacancy.

REPLY TO LETTER ASKING IF YOU WANT TO BE PUT ON WAITING LIST, WITHOUT COMMITMENT ON EITHER PART (YOUR'S OR EMPLOYER'S)

12 Park Lane,
Crispen.
Nr Alton.
A21 C734
Telephone: Alton 70132

2nd Jun 86

Mr D. Wilton,
Manager,
Soft-Toys Ltd.,
39 Parr Road,
Alton A42 1J

Dear Mr Wilton,

Thank you for your letter dated 28th May. I was disappointed at not being accepted for the job, however, I am pleased that you have written about putting me on your Waiting List.

I would still like to work for your company and hope to get the chance to do so. I will be very pleased if you put my name on your Waiting List and understand that this is without commitment on either part.

Thank you for seeing me last week.

Yours sincerely,
Peter Martin

P.S. I have showed my parents your letter and they are pleased too!

Prompt reply — natural tone (disappointed at not getting the job for which he was interviewed but still keen to work there).

HANDWRITTEN LETTER OF ACCEPTANCE OF JOB — TO BE SENT WITH SIGNED COPY OF CONTRACT OF EMPLOYMENT

30 Elm Road
Sipley
Derbyshire
SD2 OL6

4th April 86

Mr B Blunt
Manager
Y.S. Port Ltd
Sipley
S 20 4JK

Dear Mr Blunt,

Thank you for your letter dated 3rd April together with contract of employment.

I am pleased to accept your offer and have signed the copy of the Employment Contract which I enclose with this letter.

I will be pleased to report to the Personnel Department at 9 a.m. on Monday 14th April 86.

Yours sincerely,
Alice Browne

Prompt — brief — clear — polite!
Although it is not necessary to send this type of letter, it gives a good impression.

Useful Addresses

Africa Educational Trust
38 King Street, London WC2 E8JS.

Association of British Correspondence Colleges
6 Francis Grove, London SW19 4DT.

Baptist Missionary Society Programme
93 Gloucester Place, London W1H 4AA.

British Shipping Career Service
Berkshire House, 168/173 High Holborn, London EC3A 8ET.

British Volunteer Programme
2 Cambridge Terrace, London NW1 4JL.

Career Analysts
Career House, 90 Gloucester Place, London W1H 4BL.

Careers & Occupational Information Centre
Moorfoot, Sheffield S1 4PQ.

Careers & Occupational Information (Scotland)
5 Kirkloan, Corstorphine, Edinburgh EH12 7HD.

Careers Research & Advisory Centre (CRAC)
Bateman Street, Cambridge CB2 1LZ.

Central Council for Education & Training in Social Work
Derbyshire House, Saint Chad's Street, London WC1H 8AD.
West Wing, Saint David's House, Wood Street, Cardiff CF1 1ES.
9 South Saint David Street, Edinburgh EH2 2BW.
14 Malone Road, Belfast BT9 5BN.

Christian Association for Adult and Continuing Education
Fox Covert, Willen, Milton Keynes MK15 9AB.

Church Missionary Society
157 Waterloo Road, London SE1 8UU.

College of the Sea
202 Lambeth Road, London SE1 7JW.

Commonwealth Scholarship Commission
36 Gordon Square, London WC1H OPF.

Concordia (Youth Service Volunteers)
8 Brunswick Place, Hove, East Sussex BN3 1ET.

DHSS Overseas Group
Newcastle-upon-Tyne NE98 1YX.

Department of Manpower Services, Northern Ireland
Netherleigh, Massey Avenue, Belfast BT4 2JP.

Eaton Hall
Notts NU5 UKCOSA (the only LEA college specifically for overseas students)

Educational Grants Advisory Service, Family Welfare Association
501/505 Kingsland Road, London E8.

Engineering Careers Information Service
54 Clarendon Road, Watford WD1 1LB.

Exchanges Department, The British Council
65 Davies Street, London W1Y 2AA.

Further Education Information Services (FEIS)
Room 531, Elizabeth House, York Road, London SE1 7PH.
* for address of local FEIS, ask your Careers Officer.

Independent Schools Careers Organisation
12a/18a Princess Way, Camberley, Surrey GU15 3SP.

Kibbutz Representatives
1a Accommodation Road, London NW11.

Missions to Seamen
St. Michael Paternoster Royal, College Hill, London EC4R 2RL.

National Advisory Centre on Careers for Women
Drayton House, 30 Gordon Street, London WC1H OAX.

National Union of Students
461 Holloway Road, London N7 6LJ.

Northern Ireland Council for Continuing Education
Rathgael House, Balloo Road, County Down BT19 2PR.

Nursing and Health Careers Centre
121/123 Edgeware Road, London WC2 2HX.

Professional & Executive Recruitment (PER)
Head Office, Moorfoot, Sheffield S1 4PQ.
* see telephone directory for nearest PER.

Quaker Peace and Service
Friends House, Euston Road, London NW1 2BJ.

The British Hotels, Restaurants & Caterers Association
13 Cork Street, London W1X 2BX.

The Engineering Council
10 Maltravers Street, London WC2R 3ER.

Voluntary Services Overseas (VSO)
9 Belgrave Square, London SW1X 8PW.

World Community Development Service (Junior Volunteers Scheme)
27 Montague Road, Botley, Oxford OX2 9AH.

Glossary

Action Line programmes: radio or TV programmes which involve 'live' participants — people who take part without any rehearsal, speaking about some (usually controversial) major topic of the moment.

Apprenticeship: the time of training for a trade or craft, e.g. engineering, bricklaying, formally agreed between employer and employee.

Aptitude test: exercises you complete within a fixed time to discover what kind of work you are likely to do well at.

CPVE (Certificate of Pre-Vocational Education): nationally-recognised educational award given to school leavers who complete one year special pre-work training at school or college.

Citizens Advice Bureau (CAB): a national organisation with local branches, staffed by trained volunteers who give advice and help to people with problems.

Correspondence course: studying by postal communication rather than face-to-face teaching.

Counselling: service given by someone trained to advise on various matters, e.g. careers.

C.V. (Curriculum Vitae): means 'course for life' — used when applying for jobs, giving brief personal details: name, address, telephone number, age, education, qualifications, work experience, interests/hobbies.

DEVAT: a group of tests which show your verbal and numerical reasoning, and mechanical aptitude.

Employment Training: government-controlled/funded training for (a) those aged 18-59 who have been unemployed for over 6 months, and (b) people with special needs — disabled, those returning to work or seeking high tech skills to keep up with changing employment situations.

Employment/Training Service: mainly government-controlled with the Employment side staffed by civil servants who deal with matters of employment and unemployment; whilst the Training Agencies are private organisations.

Enterprise Allowance Scheme: a government-funded scheme which, providing you have £1,000, helps you set up your own small business by paying you a weekly sum for one year.

Health and Safety Regulations: legal requirements for health and safety of employees at work, as defined by the government.

Jobclub: government-funded, set up in areas of high unemployment to assist groups of long-term unemployed in concentrated job search.

Job Market: existing job vacancies.

Job specification: a brief description of job responsibilities and tasks involved.

Open Learning: flexible learning with programme tailored to suit individual needs. You can learn at your own pace at a time and place to suit you (home, work, Open College's access centres).

Personal details: (in relation to employment) basic facts about you — full name, address, telephone number, age, education, qualifications, work experience.

Personal profile: brief information about yourself.

Referee: Someone who provides a personal recommendation to support your application for a job.

Role play: taking part in an imagined situation, e.g. employment interview.

Self-employment: work for yourself — be your own boss.

Self-assessment: judging your own abilities — strong points and areas to be improved upon.

Service company: organisation which sells a service rather than manufacturing goods, e.g. insurance, banks.

Skillcentre: training workshop where you are given intensive instruction in a particular skill.

State benefits: government benefits e.g. Unemployment Benefit, or Housing Benefit — money you claim through your local Department of Social Security (DSS).

Take-home pay: net pay — the actual amount of money you take home after all deductions, e.g. Income Tax, National Insurance contributions.

TAPS (Training Access Points): helps you identify training opportunities which best meet your needs. Provides quick access to education and training information through computer-backed TAPS located in Jobcentres, public libraries and Careers Offices.

Vocational guidance: advice about work appropriate to your personal qualities and abilities.

VSO (Voluntary Service Overseas): an international organisation which employs volunteers who have suitable skills to work overseas, mostly in under-developed countries.

Youth Training: formal government training for young people.

Useful Books and Leaflets

USEFUL BOOKS

Careers Guide: Opportunities in the Professions, Industry, Commerce and the Public Service: Careers & Occupational Information Centre, Moorfoot, Sheffield, Annual.

Directory of Jobs & Careers Abroad: David Leppard.*

1986 Directory of Summer Jobs Abroad: David Woodworth.*

Directory of Summer Jobs in Britain: Susan Griffith.*

Directory of Work and Study in Developing Countries: David Leppard.*

DISABILITY rights handbook: the Disability Alliance's guide to benefits and services. Produced each year and updated 3 times a year by the Disability Rights Bulletin.

The Education Factbook. A-Z Guide to Education & Training in Britain: Macmillan.

Handbook of Scottish Central Institutions: Courses and Entry Requirements: available free from the Assistant Registrar, Paisley College of Technology, High Street, Paisley, Scotland PA1 2BE.

How to Get a Job Abroad: Roger Jones (Northcote House).

How to Live & Work in America: Steve Mills (Northcote House).

How to Live & Work in Australia: Laura Veltman (Northcote House).

How to Study Abroad: Teresa Tinsley (Northcote House).

How to Survive at College: David Acres (Northcote House).

International Directory of Voluntary Work: David Woodworth.*

Kibbutz Volunteer: John Bedford.*

Student Welfare Manual: the National Union of Students handbook; lists sources of help; particularly useful for overseas students.

1986 Summer Employment Directory of the U.S. Published by Writers' Digest Books in America and distributed in Europe by Vacation Work.

*Vacation Traineeships 1986.**

Working Abroad: Harry Brown (Northcote House).

* Vacation Work Publications, 9 Park End Street, Oxford OX1 1JH.

USEFUL LEAFLETS

The COI/Department of Employment publish a wide range of free leaflets which may be obtained from your Jobcentre or by writing to the Careers and Occupation Information Centre, Moorfoot, Sheffield. They include:

Your Guide to Our Employment, Training & Enterprise Programmes
Employment Training — The Facts
Employment Training — It's Your Future — Shape It
Employment Training for Women
Advice for those interested in Part-time Work
Jobstart — Helping you get back into work
The Enterprise Allowance Scheme
Career Development Loans
Childcare Payments for Lone Parents on Employment Training
Employment Training — Health Problem or Disability?
Jobhunting for People With Disabilities
Travel To Work Grants for People With Disabilities

The COI/Department of Education and Science publish a series of useful leaflets which are obtainable free from school or college. These include:

Choose your course
Choosing at 16
The Certificate of Pre-Vocational Education (CPVE)

The Department of Social Security (DSS) supply free informative leaflets such as:

Leaving School? A pocket guide to Social Security
Unemployment benefit

Other useful free leaflets include:

BBC Education — What kind of New Year (BBC Education).
How to Live in Britain (The British Council) — covers employment, immigration, accommodation, student life; plus list of useful addresses.
British Rail: Young Persons Railcard Offer (for those between 16 and 24 years old) — gives brief details of other schemes, discounts, etc.
OVER 16 — a useful free magazine from Girobank; usually distributed by educational establishments and libraries.
Working Abroad (Employment Service).

Index